LITTLE BOOK OF SHEFFIELD 2025

THE LITTLE BOOK OF
SHEFFIELD 2025

CONTENTS

THE BEAR

in good company.

DET

WELCOME TO

THE LITTLE BOOK OF SHEFFIELD 2025

EDITION

Well, would you look at that, it's five whole years since we published the first Little Book of Sheffield. How on earth did that happen? One minute we were tentatively stepping back into the world post-lockdown, desperate for a decent coffee, some live music and to show some much-needed support to our beleaguered independents. Then before you know it, quicker than you can mumble "Eat out to help out", we're back here again – rounding up the very best of the city's indie scene in one handy little package.

A lot's changed since 2020 (not least the number of grey hairs appearing in our beards), but what's stayed exactly the same is Sheffield's rock-solid creative spirit. This place we call home continues to buzz with passionate people doing brilliant things – chefs, brewers, artists, shopkeepers, designers, makers – and The Little Book of Sheffield 2025 is our way of celebrating them all.

As the team behind Exposed Magazine – Sheffield's go-to entertainment guide for over 20 years – we reckon we know a thing or two about what makes the city tick. So we've put those hard-earned credentials to good use – the same ones we rely on every day to sniff out the best gigs, grub and good times – to compile a fresh guide to the people and places keeping the Steel City sharp.

This isn't an exhaustive list, and it's not meant to be. It's a whistlestop tour of the areas we love and a snapshot of the indies that make them sing. From city-centre newcomers to long-standing neighbourhood legends, we'll be introducing you to a few of our favourite residents along the way – the kind of spots we send our mates to, and the kind of people we're proud to have in Sheffield.

Whether you're flicking through for weekend inspiration or plotting your own route across the city, we hope you'll find something new to love – and maybe even learn a thing or two about our wonderful city along the way.

Ash Birch and Joe Food, Exposed Magazine

S

THE LITTLE BOOK OF
SHEFFIELD 2025

CROOKES & WALKLEY

We begin our journey around the Steel City in Crookes and Walkley – two hilltop neighbourhoods where student life meets strong local roots, and the views are worth the climb.

These two neighbouring suburbs, perched above the city, are the kind of places that make you glad Sheffield isn't flat. Popular with students, young families and long-time locals alike, both Crookes and Walkley strike a winning balance between community spirit, coffee culture and a proudly independent streak.

Crookes has been a settlement for over a thousand years – once known as Krkur, a Viking word meaning "nook" – and later mentioned in the Domesday Book. Back then it was all farms and fields, but by the 1800s it had grown into a thriving village with inns, chapels and cutlers' workshops supplying the city's steel industry. These days, its main street buzzes with cafés, bakeries, pubs and takeaways – from pizzas at Paesani to carefully crafted coffees at Cloud and banging baked goods from Crumb.

Walkley shares that same spirit but has its own flavour. Built on the back of Sheffield's 19th-century growth, it was once full of steelworkers and artisans living in neat terrace rows. The Walkley of today is fiercely community-minded, with long-standing favourites like Walkley Beer Co and Gerry's Bakery sitting alongside newer names like Freak Street Café.

Both areas have seen a new wave of independents move in, often side by side with much-loved old favourites. They're lively, lived-in and properly local – a gentle start to our tour, but full of charm.

Grab a coffee and take in the view across the city from Bolehills – this is Crookes and Walkley, and it's time to meet some of its residents.

TENAYA WINE

California dreamin'

Blending West Coast cool with expert curation, Tenaya Wine offers standout bottles, weekly glass lists and tastings that make quality wine approachable for all.

Set on Crookes High Street in a former charity shop, Tenaya Wine brings a laid-back slice of California to Sheffield's hills.

Part stylish bottle shop, part relaxed bar and all about making good wine feel accessible and fun, it's fast become an important neighbourhood hangout.

Tenaya is owned by wine enthusiast Virginia Myers, who brings years of experience – both making wine in the States and running wine shops here in the UK. Named after the idyllic canyon, creek and lake in Yosemite, Tenaya reflects the friendly, unpretentious spirit of the West Coast. That means shelves full of brilliant wines, with a soft spot for California and a well-chosen range from around the world – all handpicked for flavour, sustainability and, often, female-led production.

Customers can buy to take away, stay for a glass, or pick any bottle from the shop and drink it in for a small corkage fee. There's also a short but sharp by-the-glass list covering reds, whites, orange wines, fizz and rosé, which changes every week. Snacks come courtesy of Porter Brook Deli, with build-your-own picnic boards of cheese, charcuterie and nibbles available to enjoy alongside your wine of choice.

Tenaya also runs monthly themed tastings – past editions have explored Spanish reds and Loire Valley whites – plus creative events like ceramics workshops and a seasonal Wine Club subscription, complete with curated bottles, tote bags and in-store perks.

It's not just the bottles that make Tenaya shine – it's the atmosphere and the knowledgeable, friendly service synonymous with the Californian vibe. Whether you're a seasoned wine-lover or just dipping your toes in, the space feels welcoming, warm and unintimidating. Every label is clearly marked and thoughtfully chosen, with plenty of approachable entry points for anyone looking to try something new.

Recently named Best Newcomer at the national Drinks Retailing Awards, Tenaya is putting Crookes – and Sheffield – on the map for modern, independent wine culture. Pop in for a bottle, stay for a glass or check out one of their regular events and tastings.

Tenaya Wine
239 - 241 Crookes
S10 1TF
07543 792379
@tenaya_wine
tenayawine.co.uk

naya

AESTHETE COFFEE + KITCHEN

A family affair with aesthetic flair

A much-loved, family-run neighbourhood gem, Aesthete Coffee + Kitchen serves up creative seasonal dishes, global flavours and warm hospitality across their two Sheffield cafés.

Aesthete Coffee + Kitchen is the result of a ten-year-long dream to bring together Alexa Exarcopoulos and her chef mum Jane Baxter's shared love of food, creativity and hospitality.

From a tiny space just up the road (which had an equally tricky name to get a Sheffield tongue around!), to their current sites in Walkley and Crosspool, each space brings its own flavour to the party, but both serve up a welcoming atmosphere, seasonal dishes and thoughtful design in equal measure.

The pair's backgrounds (Sheffield roots, Greek heritage) add a subtle international touch to a menu that takes inspiration from everywhere. Think brunch classics with unexpected twists – whipped avocado on sourdough toast, topped with poached eggs, pickled onion and za'atar or shakshuka-style baked 'Greek Green Eggs' with whipped feta – alongside globally influenced plates like Bombay bowls, Italian toasties and vibrant seasonal soups. Everything is made in-house, right down to the focaccia, pittas and cakes – including celebration bakes to order.

But this is far more than just a menu café. Aesthete thrives on experimentation, with up to a dozen new specials popping up each day, depending on what's in season, what's inspiring the kitchen, or even what the team are reading that week. Both Alexa and Jane are keen cookbook collectors and love deep-diving into different cuisines and eras to reimagine dishes through a fresh, homegrown lens. It's food that's playful, instinctive and made with heart – and the team's excitement to try new things is infectious.

The kitchen's creativity is most clearly seen in the specials board, where you'll find up to a dozen new dishes a day, all beautifully presented and often inspired by those cookbook deep-dives. This is food made with love and curiosity – and just the right amount of flair.

Aesthete Coffee + Kitchen
348 – 352 South Road
Walkley
S6 3TE
0114 232 2000
&
52a Sandygate Road
Crosspool
S10 5RY
0114 479 2000
@aesthete_sheffield

AESTHETE COFFEE + KITCHEN

Inside, the café lives up to the connotations of its name. Handmade artwork, carefully chosen lighting and a relaxed, organic style make sure the aesthetic is on point, while the team – warm, attentive and clearly passionate about what they do – ensure the welcome is as memorable as the meal. There's even a gallery wall featuring pieces from local artists, including some by Alexa and Jane themselves.

You'll also find design touches that reflect their personal journeys – Alexa's background in art and design is echoed throughout the space, from handpicked tableware to the printed cards and candles they sell on the counter. The walls and shelves often change depending on new ideas, collaborations, or simply the season. It's this flexibility – and the lack of corporate rules – that gives Aesthete its charm.

Outside, both cafés boast peaceful courtyard seating: a rare treat in Sheffield, and the perfect spot to soak up the good vibes with a flat white or falafel wrap. Aesthete is more than just a café – it's a creative, community-led space where every detail counts, and every visit offers something new.

And while the presentation might be beautiful, nothing about Aesthete is precious or pretentious. The team is small, friendly and fiercely welcoming – they've created a space that's equal parts neighbourhood hub and quiet sanctuary. Regulars know they can pop in solo for a midweek brunch or bring a crowd for a baby shower, book club or private event. The cafés flex to fit the people they serve – whether that's coffee to go, cake for a wedding, or a family breakfast in the garden.

With two locations and a growing loyal following, Aesthete's next chapter is already in motion – always evolving, always rooted in a love for food, family and a little creative magic.

Aesthete Coffee + Kitchen
348 – 352 South Road
Walkley
S6 3TE
0114 232 2000
&
52a Sandygate Road
Crosspool
S10 5RY
0114 479 2000
@aesthete_sheffield

BUT THIS IS FAR MORE THAN JUST A MENU CAFÉ. AESTHETE THRIVES ON EXPERIMENTATION, WITH UP TO A DOZEN NEW SPECIALS POPPING UP EACH DAY

Æsthete
COFFEE • KITCHEN

SORREL'S COCOA BAKERY

Sweet dreams are made of these

A colourful Crookes gem known for handmade chocolates, rotating fresh bakes and cult-favourite hot cookie days, all crafted in a nearby Walkley kitchen.

Sorrel's Cocoa Bakery in Crookes is a local favourite for handmade chocolates, chunky cookies and indulgent bakes. Founded by Sorrel Botham in 2014, the bakery now operates from both Crookes and Walkley, offering small-batch treats, seasonal specials and irresistible hot cookies straight from the oven.

Set in the heart of Crookes, Sorrel's Cocoa Bakery is a much-loved spot known for its chunky cookies, beautiful bakes and sumptuous sweet treats – all made by hand in small batches by a tight-knit team just down the road in Walkley.

What began as a chocolate-making hobby in 2014, sparked by a love of sweets and the desire to create something joyful, soon turned into a business, with early success at farmer's markets and pop-ups, leading owner Sorrel Botham to open her first bricks-and-mortar shop in Crookes in 2018.

With its pastel pink frontage and lovingly restored interior, the original shop quickly became a neighbourhood favourite, known for its tempting mix of handmade chocolate, fresh bakes and inventive flavours.

The Crookes shop is now open seven days a week, stocked with a rotating counter of freshly baked cookies, brownies, blondies, and celebration boxes. Their popular bon bon counter lets you build your own pick'n'mix box of handmade chocolates, with flavours changing regularly and plenty of limited-run options to try. You'll also find indulgent mixed bake boxes, pre-order treats and seasonal specials, all created with care in their Walkley kitchen.

Originally operating out of Attercliffe, the bakery recently relocated production to Walkley. Being just minutes from the Crookes shop means they can now restock easily throughout the day and proudly tell customers that everything really is made just around the corner.

Though the Walkley kitchen wasn't originally intended as a customer-facing space, the locals had other ideas. With people regularly wandering in off the street or asking what was going on inside, the team began trialling limited opening hours – and it stuck. The Walkley bakery is now open on Thursdays and Saturdays for 'hot cookie days', where customers can buy their favourite cookies straight from the oven. It's quickly become a hit, with the scent of freshly baked chocolate drawing people in from the street.

Sorrel's Cocoa Bakery
158 Crookes S10 1UH
&
192 – 194 Howard Road
Walkley
S6 3RX
@sorrelscocoabakery

£4.25
Raspberry
£4.50
Biscoff Caramel Rocky Road
£4.50

If you don't have anything nice to say, eat more cookies until you do.
Biscoff Caramel
Double
Sorrel's Cocoa Bakery

Build Your Own Hamper
1. Pick a box.
2. Choose your flavours from the shelves.
3. We'll pack it for you.

Sorrel's Cocoa Bakery
FINE CHOCOLATE & BAKES
You look like you need some chocolate

THE LITTLE BOOK OF
SHEFFIELD 2025

HILLSBOROUGH

Just down the hill from Walkley you arrive in Hillsborough – a proudly working-class neighbourhood in the north-west that has seen a recent revival of quality independents bring new life to the area. Born from the city's industrial boom, the S6 suburb grew into a bustling neighbourhood built on steel, trams and terrace houses – and over the years, it's held onto that no-nonsense charm.

Of course, no mention of the area would be complete without a nod to its football team. Sheffield Wednesday (other Sheffield football clubs are, of course, available) and Hillsborough Stadium have resided here for well over a century, bringing passion, local pride and plenty of noise every matchday. And then there's the leafy Hillsborough Park – a proper Sheffield gem and home to the city's biggest music bash, Tramlines. Each summer, huge acts and thousands of revellers descend on the neighbourhood for three days of tunes and good vibes.

That said, Hillsborough hasn't always made headlines for the right reasons. It's an area that's had its share of difficult moments, most notably the tragedy that changed football forever in the 1980s. But resilience runs deep here and in recent years, Hillsborough has been quietly reworking its story.

There's a buzz about the place now. A wave of new independents has brought fresh energy to Middlewood Road, in particular – cafés, delis, bars, bakeries, flower shops and lifestyle stores sitting side by side with long-standing locals. It's still the Hillsborough you remember – you can still get an award-winning banger from F. Funk's butchers – but you can now also grab a banging flat white from one of the welcoming new cafés.

So, jump on a Yellow tram towards Middlewood and get off at Hillsborough Corner – we're continuing our tour where tradition meets reinvention. Let's meet some of the residents adding fresh flavour to one of Sheffield's most storied suburbs...

BORN FROM THE CITY'S INDUSTRIAL BOOM, THE S6 SUBURB GREW INTO A BUSTLING NEIGHBOURHOOD BUILT ON STEEL, TRAMS AND TERRACE HOUSES

Tramlines photo: Matt Higgs

TRAMLINES

RELISH

ANNIE JUDE'S

Shopping small, supporting local

Annie Jude's on Middlewood Road is a Hillsborough favourite, offering handmade gifts, homeware and small-batch treats from UK makers. Founded by Faith Nicholson in memory of her mum, the award-winning shop celebrates creativity, community and the joy of shopping small.

If you're gift hunting in S6, Annie Jude's is the go-to. A warm and welcoming independent on Middlewood Road, this carefully curated shop has become a much-loved part of Hillsborough's indie high street – and with good reason.

Run by the wonderfully passionate Faith Nicholson and her small team, Annie Jude's offers a joyful mix of handmade products, small-batch treats and beautifully crafted gifts from UK makers – the majority Sheffield-based and many female-led. Whether you're after a thoughtful card, a pampering pick-me-up or something stylish for the home, the shelves are full of ideas you didn't know you needed – until you walk in.

Named in memory of Faith's late mum, Judith Anne, the shop was set up in the aftermath of Covid – born from a desire to support makers she'd discovered online during lockdown and to channel her own creative spark. That passion for people and place runs through everything here – from the friendly atmosphere to strong community ties and regular collaborations with fellow small businesses.

Candles, prints, ceramics, skincare, jewellery, sweet treats, textiles, stationery – it's a treasure trove of useful, joyful and sustainable gifting. Stock changes regularly, with plenty of one-offs and limited runs, so there's always something new to discover. And if you're lucky, you might time your visit with a maker pop-up, creative collab or late-night shopping event.

Voted Best Independent Shop at the Exposed Awards in 2023, Annie Jude's is a reminder of what shopping small is all about: connection, creativity and a genuine love for the neighbourhood it calls home.

Annie Jude's
92 Middlewood Road
Hillsborough
S6 4HA
@anniejudesshop

LOVE IS LOVE

BE REYT
CHUFFIN FREEZIN

Claymore Candles
Fig & Cassis
Wax Melts £4 each or 3 for £10
Sandalwood
Claymore Candle.Co
SANDALWOOD
Wax Melts £4 each or 3 for £10

WEDNESDAY
UNITED
Reyt team.

THE ORANGE BIRD

The future's bright...

The Orange Bird brings South African flair to Sheffield dining. Run by chef Matt Duggan-Jones and host Anne Horner, it combines flame-fired cooking, warm hospitality and a sense of community.

In the heart of Hillsborough, The Orange Bird blends South African influences with modern, inventive cooking to create a dining experience unlike anything else in Sheffield.

Co-owned by chef Matt Duggan-Jones – who draws on his South African heritage – and front-of-house host Anne Horner, this small but vibrant neighbourhood restaurant has built its reputation on the pair's complementary skillsets: Matt's bold, flame-fired cooking and Anne's warm, effortless hospitality.

Having opened in November 2020 – amid the challenges of lockdown – The Orange Bird has been on a journey of adaptation that's shaped everything about the intimate dining spot. The food, the service, and the sense of community at the heart of the restaurant have all grown naturally over time, shaped more by passion than by following trends.

Matt's menu is rooted in the memories and methods of his upbringing – think cooking over wood, smoky spices, nostalgic desserts – but filtered through the lens of his fine-dining experience. When he first fired up the braai for a themed night, it sparked something special: a return to childhood flavours, reimagined with modern skill and care. Since then, the offering has evolved, from the ever-popular peri peri chicken to inventive seasonal dishes that balance boldness with finesse.

Anne, meanwhile, ensures every guest feels at home the moment they walk through the door. Her attention to detail, knowledge of the menu and knack for creating a relaxed, welcoming atmosphere have made her the heart of the dining room. Together, she and Matt have shaped a restaurant that feels both refined and familiar – a place where regulars are greeted by name and newcomers soon become friends.

The drinks list complements the experience, with South African wines, beers and whiskies sitting alongside handcrafted cocktails and the occasional bottle of mezcal. Many diners travel from afar for nostalgic favourites like the Peppermint Crisp tart, while locals treat it as their go-to neighbourhood spot.

The Orange Bird isn't about formality or fuss – it's about great food, genuine warmth and a shared love of good company. It may take inspiration from South Africa, but the result is entirely its own – a celebration of personal heritage, technique and community.

The Orange Bird
78 Middlewood Road
Hillsborough
S6 4HA
0114 234 9330
@theorangebirdcanteen

Pictures: Ellie Grace Photography

CHOKING

the
Orange
Bird

THE GREEN SHOP

Green shoots for a 21st-century corner shop

A Hillsborough institution reimagined for today, The Green Shop blends the warmth of a traditional corner shop with the spirit of a modern community hub.

A familiar landmark for Hillsborough locals, The Green Shop stands proudly on the corner of Wadsley Lane and Marlcliffe Road, doing what Sheffield's best shops have always done – serving the community with quality produce and bringing people together.

Despite being officially named GR GR Granvilles for decades, the shop was always affectionately known as The Green Shop – a reference point, meeting spot, and social hub for generations. Reimagined in 2020 by current custodians Sam and Anne Grayson – who finally gave it a name to match its iconic green frontage – they've honoured its heritage while reshaping it for a new era: part corner shop, part café, part deli, all heart.

Inside, the offer is wide-ranging but well-curated: hearty sandwiches, toasties, pies and scotch eggs line the counter, alongside cheeses, sauces, chutneys and bakes from a rotating cast of brilliant local bakeries. The coffee's excellent, there's always something tempting among the sweet treats, and they've somehow managed to make the school run feel suitably bougie!

As well as the newer additions, the essentials remain front and centre – fresh fruit and veg stacked in wooden crates, a carefully chosen range of beers and wines lining the back walls and fridges, and, for the kids (and big kids among us), the penny sweets, that have been a shop staple for decades, can still be scooped into paper bags – because some things never change.

The shop proudly champions Sheffield's independent makers too, with shelves in the back dedicated to locally made art, cards, gifts, and homeware, as well as an environmentally conscious refill section perfect for topping up cereals, jars of pasta, or cleaning products.

And while it's easy to pop in for a quick lunch or a pint of milk, The Green Shop's real magic lies in its atmosphere. People bump into each other, stop to chat, and linger over coffee. It's the kind of place where the school run turns into a mini social gathering, and no one's in too much of a rush.

The name might be new(ish), but the soul of the place – that old-fashioned, communal buzz – has been here for years.

The Green Shop
128 Wadsley Lane
S6 4ED
07919 593041
@thegreenshopsheffield

SHOP

the Real
OF CHESTERFIELD

LICENSED TO SELL TOBACCO

MOLLY'S CAFÉ & DELI

Hillsborough's homegrown hospitality heroes

A Hillsborough favourite, Molly's Café & Deli is a family-run gem known for its warmth, creativity and Polish-inspired flair. Founded by Lucy and Piotr Poplawski, it's a place where homemade food and heartfelt hospitality make every visit feel like coming home.

A true Hillsborough success story, Molly's Café & Deli has fast become one of Sheffield's most beloved foodie spots. Run by husband-and-wife team Lucy and Piotr Poplawski – along with their four children and amazing team – this family-run café on Middlewood Road is known for its warmth, charm and queues that often stretch down the street, whatever the weather.

Molly's opened just one day before the pandemic forced cafés to close – but what could've been a disaster quickly turned into something special. Pivoting to home deliveries of cheese and charcuterie boards (with a signature Polish twist), the family built a loyal following overnight. Today, that side hustle has grown into a thriving outside catering business serving up to 1,000 people a week, with artisan platters gracing everything from weddings to corporate boardrooms.

In the café itself, everything is made fresh to order with a big emphasis on quality, creativity and zero waste. Piotr heads up the savoury side, infusing the menu with Slavic flavours and deli favourites, while Lucy's homemade cakes and bakes regularly stop passers-by in their tracks. Whether it's a Polish Smoked Sausage & Egg Bap, a homemade sausage roll or a slice of something sweet, you're guaranteed something delicious and just a little bit different.

The café has become a catalyst for Hillsborough's indie food scene, helping to revive this corner of S6 and attracting a community of like-minded neighbours. There's something undeniably special about Molly's: the feeling that you've stumbled on a place where food is made with love, family is at the heart of everything and the welcome is as warm as the coffee.

Molly's Café & Deli
93 Middlewood Road
Hillsborough
S6 4GX
07925 432394
@mollyscafeanddeli

Molly's Deli
COFFEE - CAKE
WINE - CHEESE
MOLLY'S
EST 2020

BURTON STREET FOUNDATION

Community, creativity and care

Burton Street Foundation is a beacon of community and creativity. Supporting people of all abilities while housing cafés, studios and local enterprises, it's a place where inclusion, imagination and Sheffield spirit come together under one welcoming roof.

Tucked away in Hillsborough, Burton Street Foundation is one of Sheffield's most quietly brilliant institutions. Housed in a cluster of beautifully preserved Victorian buildings, it's not just a community hub – it's a vibrant, inclusive space where creativity thrives and people have come together for over 25 years.

At its core, Burton Street is all about people. The charitable not-for-profit organisation supports over 250 adults and young people with learning disabilities, physical disabilities, autism and mental health conditions. Their approach is person-led, vibrant and full of heart – built around creative sessions, proper community connection and the belief that everyone deserves to live their happiest, most fulfilled life.

Inside the walls, you'll find a buzzing, colourful world. Drama classes, baking groups, dance troupes and songwriting sessions spill out into corridors decorated with art and full of life. Some days there's a filmmaking crew, others you'll stumble into a sensory chill-out zone or a five-a-side match. No two days look the same – and that's the point.

It's not just the day-to-day that's unique – it's the culture. Since opening in 1998, Burton Street has built a workplace where talent, compassion and creativity thrive. The team is handpicked not just for their experience, but for their spark – carers and staff who bring as much energy and joy to the place as the people they support.

With a second site now running in Beighton, the Burton Street story continues to grow. But the heart of it all remains the same – an inclusive space where support means more than services, and where 'Everyone Has A Part To Play'.

Burton Street Foundation
57 Burton Street
Hillsborough
S6 2HH
0114 233 2908
@burtonstreetfoundation
burtonstreet.org.uk

EVERYONE
HAS
A PART
TO PLAY

A SPACE FOR SHEFFIELD

Meeting rooms, flat whites, weddings and workshops

Burton Street Foundation isn't just a community organisation – it's a destination. Alongside their incredible support services, the site is also home to some of Sheffield's most flexible and welcoming spaces, all rooted in the ethos that people do their best when they feel connected.

The café is the beating heart of the place. Open Monday to Friday, 9.00am to 3.30pm, it serves proper coffee, delicious meals and freshly baked treats – all made and served with care by a team of staff, volunteers and people supported by Burton Street. It's the kind of space where community groups gather, old friends catch up, and strangers soon become regulars.

Need a space to hire? You're spoiled for choice. Function rooms range from intimate setups to full-on party spaces for up to 120 guests – ideal for birthdays, weddings, charity events or local meet-ups. They're accessible, welcoming and properly equipped, with in-house catering, a licensed bar and free parking on-site.

For something a little more formal, there are slick conference rooms with all the AV kit and breakout space you'd need for team sessions, seminars or business events. There's also dedicated space for networking and training, offering flexible layouts, collaborative corners and a friendly feel that encourages real connection.

Then there's the office space. Bright, characterful rooms with Victorian features, skylights and secure access – a perfect base for start-ups or small teams looking for fruitful co-working. And because it's Burton Street, renting space here means giving back too – every booking helps support their disability services and community work.

Whether you're planning a big do, launching a business or just fancy a sausage roll and a cuppa, Burton Street Foundation is the kind of place that makes things happen – a true Sheffield gem with space for everyone.

Burton Street Foundation
57 Burton Street
Hillsborough
S6 2HH
0114 233 2908
@burtonstreetfoundation
burtonstreet.org.uk

Right: A Makaton lesson from clients of Burton Street Foundation

Yes
BEND WRIST

No

Thank you
SHORT

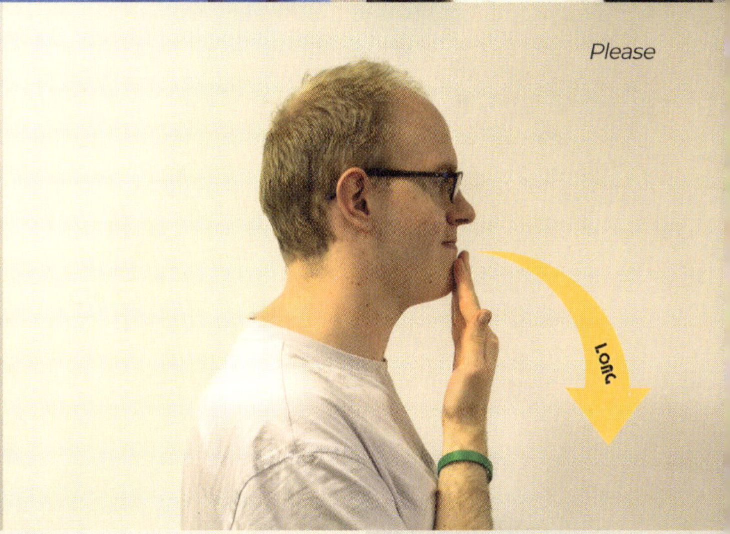
Please
LONG

Help

Home

THE LITTLE BOOK OF
SHEFFIELD 2025

KELHAM ISLAND & NEEPSEND

Just a short hop from Hillsborough, the tour rolls into Neepsend and neighbouring Kelham Island – two old industrial districts that, thanks to the hard work of ambitious business owners, have been reinvented over the last couple of decades. Once the beating heart of Sheffield's steel industry, this area was all clanking machinery, smoke-belching chimneys and heavy graft. Today? Let's just say it scrubs up well.

The bones of that industrial past are still proudly on show – think cobbled lanes, old factories and towering brick warehouses – but these days, they're housing some of the best bars, restaurants and creative spaces the city has to offer. It's a collision of old and new, where heritage buildings play host to everything from mezcal bars to microbreweries, stylish apartments and hidden-away galleries.

It's no wonder Kelham was recently named the coolest neighbourhood in the UK by Time Out. The area's mix of grit, character and charm has won it plenty of admirers. The mighty Kelham Island Museum still tells the story of Sheffield's steel roots, while old-school boozers like The Fat Cat and Kelham Island Tavern continue to pull perfect pints as they've done for decades.

Meanwhile, Neepsend (a little further up the road and often subsumed by Kelham Island's popularity) is making its own name, with venues like Alder, Church and Factory Floor helping shift the city's nightlife up a gear. The whole area buzzes with creative energy, and Yellow Arch Studios, the old practice rooms once frequented by a certain Arctic Monkeys, continue to house local bands as a live music venue.

It's a place where you're just as likely to stumble upon a punk gig as you are a Sunday roast worth writing home about. So sit down for a pint, and meet some of the brilliant independents that make Kelham Island and Neepsend tick...

THESE DAYS THEY'RE HOUSING SOME OF THE BEST BARS, RESTAURANTS AND CREATIVE SPACES THE CITY HAS TO OFFER

Warmth Sauna image: Ellie Grace Photography

CAMPARI

MOMA

DOMO

Sardinian soul food

Bringing Sardinian flavour and heartfelt hospitality to Eagle Works, Domo is a beloved Italian restaurant that offers authentic dishes, relaxed courtyard dining and a true home-from-home feel to Kelham.

Found on the ground floor of the heritage-listed Eagle Works building in Kelham Island, Domo brings a much-welcomed dash of Sardinian sunshine to Sheffield's dining scene.

Since opening in summer 2019, it's become a firm favourite for leisurely weekend meals or after-work aperitivos where punters snack on pizza, bruschetta and olives washed down with Italian beers or Aperol Spritz.

Step through the doors and you're transported straight to the Mediterranean. The bright, spacious interior blends rustic charm with regional flair – Sardinian masks, handwoven baskets and greenery setting the scene for relaxed, authentic dining. Outside, a sun-drenched courtyard hums with chatter as plates and glasses circulate late into the evening.

The restaurant is run by partners Sarah Elliott and Raffaelle Busceddu, whose family roots stretch back to Castelsardo, an idyllic coastal town in northern Sardinia. When Domo opened, family members came from Italy to lend a hand – a gesture that set the tone for the heartfelt hospitality that's defined the venue ever since. "Domo" translates to "home," and everything here, from the food to the welcome, captures that spirit.

Menus celebrate the breadth of Sardinian cuisine with sections devoted to dishes from the land and from the sea, showcasing regional recipes passed down through generations. Expect comforting classics made with fresh, seasonal ingredients and served with an easy, familial warmth – food that feels both refined and refreshingly unpretentious.

At its heart, Domo is a love letter to Sardinia: a place where food, family and friendship intertwine. Whether you're popping in for coffee, gathering for a long lunch or sipping cocktails in the courtyard, it's the kind of spot that makes you linger – a true home from home in Kelham.

Domo
Eagle Works
34-36 Cotton Mill Walk
Little Kelham
S3 8DH

@domosheffield

Pictures: @elliegracephotography and @kelhamstudio

DOMO

Cassola Zu Raffellu

"This classic Sardinian fish stew was my grandad's pride – a seaside ritual in Castelsardo whenever I came home for the holidays. Made with the freshest catch, tomatoes, garlic, and a splash of white wine, his secret was patience: letting the sea's flavour slowly marry with the sauce."

Preparation time: 10 minutes | Cooking time: 10 minutes | Serves: 2–4

Ingredients:

70g extra virgin olive oil
100g onion, chopped
2 garlic cloves, chopped
5g chilli flakes
14g parsley, chopped
1 can San Marzano tomatoes
120ml dry white wine
250ml fish and crustacean broth
1.2kg mixed seafood (red snapper, swordfish, Argentinian king prawns, stone bass, baby squid)
6 slices ciabatta bread, toaste
1 garlic clove, for rubbing the toast
salt and black pepper, to season

Method:

Heat the olive oil in a large heavy pot over medium heat. Add the onion and sauté for 2 minutes, then add the garlic and chilli flakes, cooking for 1 minute.

Stir in the parsley, tomatoes and white wine. Strain the fish and crustacean broth into the pot, stir well and simmer for 5 minutes.

Clean the baby squid and prawns, and cut the fish into quarters.

Add the squid to the pot and season with salt and pepper. Cook for 8–10 minutes, until just firm but not rubbery.

Add the remaining seafood and simmer for a further 10 minutes until everything is cooked through.

Rub the toasted ciabatta with a clove of garlic and serve alongside the stew in bowls.

Domo
Eagle Works
34–36 Cotton Mill Walk
Little Kelham
S3 8DH

@domosheffield

Pic: Ellie Grace Photography.

MERCHANTS HOUSE

Continental vibes with a Kelham twist

European-style bar meets Kelham cool, with an impressive range of spritzes, Spanish small plates and serious wine game.

From the team behind Alder – the beloved Kelham bar known for its laidback vibes and community spirit – comes Merchants House, a stylish new venue that's already making waves in Merchants Court on Mowbray Street. While Alder leans into cosy charm, Merchants takes a more polished approach, channelling a European bistro feel with sharp cocktails, quality wines and ever-evolving small plates.

Step through the courtyard space and you'll find a modern, light-filled space with a breezy, social atmosphere. There's seating for all sorts – intimate tables for two, roomy booths for group catch-ups – and plenty of outdoor space for spritz season in full swing. A separate events room situated opposite the bar is geared up to host everything from supper clubs to creative workshops.

On the menu, it's all about doing the simple things well. Small plates start from just a couple of quid, with favourites including boquerones on crisp baguette, spicy cider-braised chorizo and baked camembert with thick-cut bread. There's also Gouda with Dijon and celery salt – oddly brilliant and seriously moreish. It's the sort of menu that encourages lingering, sharing and ordering one more 'for the table'.

Behind the bar, you're spoilt for choice. Fifteen wines by the glass keep things interesting, while a tight cocktail list focuses on continental classics with a twist – Negronis, Americanos, Martinis and a sharp Paloma all feature. For fans of the fizzy stuff, there's a rotating Spritz of the Week and five house varieties, from Limoncello to Lillet Rose, all sitting comfortably under a tenner.

And beer hasn't been forgotten either. Twelve taps pour everything from continental lagers to local favourites, while an impressive selection of ciders, draught wines and a well-stocked bottle fridge means all tastes are catered for.

With a clear vision and clever execution, Merchants House brings something fresh to Kelham's ever-growing food and drink scene. Whether you're in for date night, a casual spritz or a full grazing session, it's a place that balances style with substance – and already feels like part of the neighbourhood.

Merchants House
Merchants Court
43 Mowbray St
S3 8EN

@merchants_house_s3

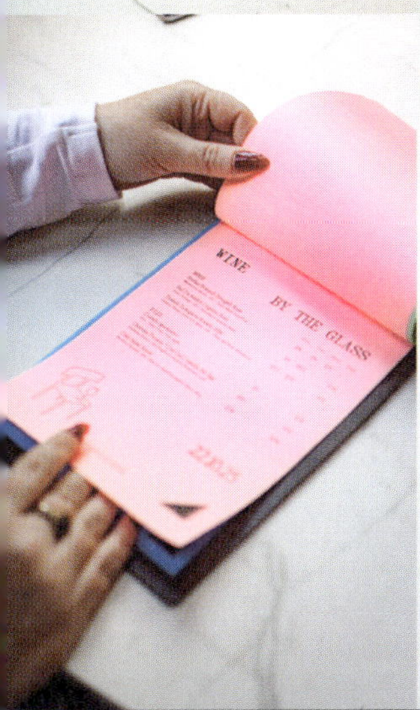
WINE
BY THE GLASS

CAMPARI

PAD 12

A hidden gem with laidback charm

Created by Dan and Laura Hall, Pad 12 is a relaxed and welcoming spot in Kelham Island – a place where the details are thoughtful, the mood is easy and everyone feels like a regular.

Tucked away among the growing collection of independents housed at Merchants Court, Pad 12 has fast become one of Kelham Island's most inviting hangouts. Open since the end of 2024, the bar came into its own over the summer months, earning a loyal following for its relaxed atmosphere, friendly faces and perfectly balanced drinks list.

Run by husband-and-wife team Dan and Laura Hall, Pad 12 is a true labour of love. What began as a bare industrial unit is now a warm, welcoming space with an easygoing personality that reflects its owners' approach. The pair designed and fitted the bar themselves, creating a venue that feels instantly familiar – somewhere between a city bolthole and your favourite local.

Inside, it's intimate and unfussy, spread across two levels with space for small groups and private gatherings. Step outside, though, and you'll find one of Kelham's best suntraps. Sheltered from the wind but bathed in light, the courtyard quickly fills on bright afternoons, turning Pad 12 into an oasis of calm amid the area's buzz.

At the bar you'll find a drinks offering that is thoughtful but unpretentious. Rotating draught beers and spirits sit alongside a well-rounded cocktail list, with early bird drinks deals and a regularly changing wine of the month thrown into the mix.

With room for around 60 to 70 guests, including the courtyard, Pad 12 is also carving out a name as a go-to spot for birthdays, engagements and laid-back weddings. Its mix of comfort, style and personal service makes it feel like a home away from home – the kind of place where you drop in for one drink and stay all afternoon.

Sunshine or not, Pad 12 brings an easy, unforced warmth to Kelham Island – a small bar with a big heart that has quickly become part of the fabric of the neighbourhood.

Pad 12
Merchant's Court
43 Mowbray St
S3 8EN

@pad12sheffield

BROOKLYN
ANGELO
PORETTI

WE SUPPORT
KELHAM PRIDE'25

GROKE COFFEE

Independent coffee with purpose

Founded by Tom and Abby, it blends Melbourne-inspired coffee culture with community values. Expect creative brunches, standout bakes and ethical coffee, all served in a warm, plant-filled space.

Since opening in early 2025, Groke Coffee has fast become one of Kelham's most talked-about cafés. Founded by Tom and Abby, both long-time hospitality hands, it's their first venture into ownership and a reflection of everything they believe a modern café should be – welcoming, fair and community-minded.

Tom trained as a barista in Melbourne and has brought a touch of that Antipodean café culture back to Sheffield. The menu leans into relaxed brunch classics with a twist – think perfectly poached eggs, hearty vegan plates (smashed edamame and pea toast, anyone?), stacked lunchtime burgers and all-day sourdough toasties. Almost everything can be made gluten-free, something close to Tom's heart, and head chef Joe brings his own flair to the kitchen, creating seasonal menus that balance comfort with creativity.

Abby leads the baking, turning out fresh treats each week that regulars can't get enough of – from the much-loved Rocky Road to matcha pistachio cookies the size of your head. On the drinks front, Extract Coffee Roasters provide the house espresso, with rotating guest and filter coffees from ethical independent roasters across the UK. For those keen to learn more, Groke's retail shelves are lined with beans that you can take home, along with information on sourcing, transparency and flavour.

The space itself is a reflection of their commitment to creating a laidback but quietly social venue – plants hanging from every corner, nature prints on the walls and big communal tables that encourage conversation. Out back, a terrace overlooks the River Don and Kelham Island Museum, the perfect suntrap for enjoying an iced matcha or a cold Triple Point beer.

Built with care rather than profit in mind, the ethos centres on looking after staff – championing fair wages, reasonable hours and sparking genuine connection. With workshops, craft events and plans for board-game socials, it's already become a popular gathering point for locals. More than just a coffee shop, Groke reflects its founders' belief that welcoming spaces can build better communities.

Groke Coffee
1A Kelham Square
S3 8RY

grokecoffee.co.uk
@groke.coffee

DRINKS
SPECIALS

CAKES
COOKIES
FLAPJACKS
COFFEE
HOT CHOCOLATE
HERBAL TEAS

NOMA

ALDER

Pulling up trees in Neepsend

Alder in Neepsend is an award-winning independent bar rooted in community and creativity. Founded by Joe Spriggs and Danny Tennant, it's known for rare beers, live music and collaborations with local makers.

In a neighbourhood brimming with boozers, Alder has carved out something special – a fiercely independent bar with community at its core and creativity running from its roots.

Tucked away on Percy Street in a repurposed redbrick former polish factory, Alder is the brainchild of Hillsborough locals Joe Spriggs and Danny Tennant. But this isn't just their venture – it's shaped by the entire team, each member leaving a personal imprint on the space, the service, and the experience. What started in 2021 as a low-key takeover has flourished into one of the city's most loved watering holes, crowned Best Bar at the Exposed Awards in 2024.

The ethos is simple: great drinks, warm welcomes and space to try new things. That freedom translates into a constantly evolving experience – whether that's a rotating selection of rare beers, imports you won't find anywhere else in the city, or collaborations with indie producers from across the UK and beyond.

The bar's programming spans weekly live music – from jazz and blues to indie, punk, metal and electronica – as well as regular DJ sets, a weekly quiz night and autism-friendly socials. There's even a free pint for every bag of street litter collected. Outside, a community herb garden – maintained by Percy St. CIC, a local org supporting young neurodivergent people – invites visitors to pick what they need, with surplus donated to the Zest Centre.

Then there's the space itself: full of character and layered with history, from the old fittings woven into the décor to hand-built furniture and rotating artwork by Sheffield creatives. Every detail tells a story – a living love letter to local.

Whether you're here for a pint, a party or a midweek chinwag, Alder is the kind of bar that makes you feel at home – and keeps you coming back for what's next.

Alder
Percy Street
Neepsend
S3 8BT
07774 760350

@alder_bar_sheff

ALDER
J.W.
Augustiner
Bräu München
gegründet 1328

STELLA ARTOIS
BEAMISH
Genuine
IRISH STOUT
THE KERNEL
INDIA PALE ALE

ALDER

J.W.
Augustiner
Bräu München

THE IN GOOD

Because life's better in good company

Founded by two best friends with a vision to create an inspiring space for the women of Sheffield, The In Good brings beautifully created events to Kelham.

Far from your average supper club, The In Good brings the women of Sheffield together for beautifully curated evenings of great food, honest conversation and meaningful connection.

Founded by best friends Nic Sowden and Rachel Hirst, the events were created to offer something inclusive, enriching and uniquely Sheffield – a space where women could meet, share experiences and feel part of something real. Held predominantly at The Mowbray, guests are welcomed with a seasonal cocktail before settling in at long communal tables for a two-course sharing-style meal, designed to spark effortless connection and conversation – whether you're arriving solo or with friends.

Guests range in age from their 20s to their 70s and come from all walks of life – NHS workers, creatives, parents, business owners and everything in between. Whether it's your first time or your fifth, you'll find yourself sitting next to someone with a story worth sharing – and a warm welcome waiting.

What sets The In Good apart is its purposeful focus. Each event spotlights a speaker panel of diverse, brilliant women sharing stories rooted in real experience – careers, creativity, health, ambition, joy and all the beautiful chaos in between. There are no name tags, no Q&As, no awkward networking vibes – just honest, uplifting talk in a room full of people who get it.

Alongside the speakers, the team collaborates with a host of female-founded businesses – from illustrators to florists – to create an immersive, visually stunning space. It's as much about celebrating local talent as it is about taking time to appreciate life's simple pleasures – delicious food and drink, beautiful surroundings and, of course, good company.

It's social, not corporate. Intentional, not transactional. And for many attendees, genuinely transformative – the kind of evening that leaves you feeling nourished in every sense and quietly stays with you long after the last glass is cleared.

The In Good
@theingood
www.theingood.co.uk

Pics: Top left: Mad About Saffron; Middle left: Alexandra Wallace Photography; Bottom left: Helen Rose Photography; Bottom right: Ellie Grace Photography.

in
good
company.

NOMAD MAISON

Nomad Maison and WARMTH bring creativity and calm to Sheffield's inner city area. Nomad Maison curates handmade homewares from African and Turkish artisans, while next door, WARMTH offers an inclusive Finnish-style sauna - two spaces united by craft, culture and community.

Located on Stanley Street, in an unassuming spot just off the Wicker and a short walk from Kelham Island, Nomad Maison has proved itself a vibrant new addition to Sheffield's creative scene. Step inside and you'll find a beautiful collection of rugs, ceramics, mirrors and soft furnishings – each piece carefully chosen and rich with story.

The shop is the vision of Jake and Yasemin, whose African and Turkish roots shape both the aesthetic and the ethos of the space. Every item is sourced directly from artisans in these regions, with a strong focus on responsible trade and traditional craftsmanship. Profits are reinvested back into the communities they work with, supporting village economies and helping preserve centuries-old techniques in weaving, loom work and ceramics.

But Nomad Maison is more than a homeware shop. It has also become a welcoming events space – a welcoming hub for emerging creatives and regularly used by local charities and social causes. Blending beauty, heritage and purpose, this small space is making a big impact – rooted in connection and built with care.

WARMTH COMMUNITY SAUNA

Based at the same address, WARMTH Community Sauna offers something special – a Finnish-style horsebox sauna bringing accessible, inclusive heat therapy to Sheffield.

This mobile sauna experience is more than just hot air. With eucalyptus and birch-infused Aufguss steam, a refreshing cold shower and plunge, and traditional birch whisks to stimulate circulation, WARMTH is a full sensory reset. It's elemental – come rain or shine – and quietly radical in its simplicity: a small timber box, heated to over 80°C, becomes a space for reflection, reconnection and community.

Founded on the belief that sauna should be for everyone, WARMTH hosts a diverse programme of sessions, including Babes in Arms, silent sessions and trans+/non-binary slots, alongside private bookings and collaborations. Regular events include sound baths and supper clubs with Nomad Maison.

Nomad Maison & Warmth Community Sauna
18 Stanley Street
S3 8HJ
@nomadmaison
nomadmaison.com
@warmthsauna
warmthsauna.co.uk

Photos: Left: Nat Luk; Top Right & Bottom right: Ellie Grace Photography

THE LITTLE BOOK OF
SHEFFIELD 2025

CITY CENTRE

We arrive at the city centre – the beating heart of the city. At first glance, you might spot the cranes and construction hoardings but look closer and you'll find a city in the thick of a proper glow-up.

Sheffield's centre has always had character – that mix of brutalist landmarks, grand old theatres and a river or two running beneath your feet. But in recent years, there's been a shift. Big ideas, bold architecture and a surge of independents have taken root among the concrete. The result? A city centre that's starting to feel like a proper destination again – not just somewhere you pass through.

We've split this section into five parts to help you get your bearings. First up: Heart of the City – a major regeneration project that's reshaping the space from Barker's Pool down to Moorhead. Expect flagship names, eye-catching buildings and some cracking indies holding their own alongside the big players.

Then there's Pubs and Bars, which you'll find dotted through backstreets, down alleys and behind unmarked doors. This is where Sheffield's after-hours personality shines – all real ale, disco balls and smoky whiskies.

Food comes next – everything from cosy cafés to destination restaurants. Whether you're on the hunt for handmade pasta dishes, locally roasted coffee or a table to mark something special, the city centre's culinary scene is stacked.

We've also made room for the city's cultural core. Landmarks is where you'll find stories in stone – the theatres, galleries, cathedral and museums that make Sheffield more than just a good night out.

And last but not least, a mention for the entertainment on offer in the city centre – from escape rooms to gameshow bars, there's plenty to do when you're not eating, drinking, or exploring the city's cultural hotspots.

This is a city centre with layers – a place that's changing fast, but still proudly Sheffield underneath. Stick with us as we dive in and meet the places, faces and flavours that give the town its heart.

BIG IDEAS, BOLD ARCHITECTURE AND A SURGE OF INDEPENDENTS HAVE TAKEN ROOT AMONG THE CONCRETE.

Kapitol Photo: Victoria Greensmith

Atelier

LEAH'S YARD

Here's what's bringing the boys (and girls) to the yard

Reimagining historic workshops for today's makers, Leah's Yard is a lovingly restored historic space where independent makers, retailers and creatives are bringing new life to old workshops.

In the heart of Sheffield city centre sits Leah's Yard, a beautifully restored Grade II listed collection of workshops once home to the city's little mesters and now transformed into a dynamic retail, food and creative space that nods to the past while bustling with modern life.

Built in the early 19th century for shear-making, tool work and silver stamping, Leah's Yard has been reimagined as a place where independent businesses, artisans and food pioneers come together to celebrate Sheffield's character and craftsmanship.

Today, the courtyard rings with a new kind of trade – indie stores and creative start-ups sharing the same DNA as those original cutlers, but with fresh vision and purpose. Part of the Heart of the City II development, the yard has brought life back to spaces that were once silent, offering affordable workspace, vibrant retail and a home for forward-thinking brands to thrive.

Leah's Yard is more than a shopping destination – it's a story of renewal, of heritage rewritten, and of Sheffield's creative future being built on its industrial roots. Wander through its brick arches and you'll find a host of businesses, each with its own identity – from an art gallery and a bookshop to a craft beer bar and a sustainable fashion studio. It's Sheffield's independent spirit under one roof, quietly bold and proudly local.

Turn the page to meet the residents putting in the hard yards to bring it all to life.

Leah's Yard
20 – 22 Cambridge Street
S1 4HP
0114 221 1811
leahsyard.com
@leahsyard

LEAH'S YARD
BEER
COCKTAILS

dão
LA COMARCAL

Gravel Pit
PLANTS • MUSIC
ART • FUN THINGS

We're Open

CRYO
JAIPUR
MIND THE FOX
INDIE RABBLE
ARBOR
HAPPY Christmas
Red Planet
ASTRAL VOYAGE
DURATION
THOMAS HARDY'S ALE
BOLLEKE
Polly's
THE KERNEL

good books
& other essentials
La Biblioteka

THE BOOKSELLER

Good books – that's the simple ethos behind La Biblioteka, an independent shop curating everything from fashion and philosophy to fantasy fiction and beautifully made stationery. Founded nearly a decade ago by Alex Maxwell with an original focus on magazines and design, it has since evolved into a space where stories, objects and art come together. Expect shelves stacked with considered titles, a growing children's section, contemporary gifts, and a gallery wall showcasing risograph prints and small-press work. With its global outlook and fresh perspective, La Biblioteka brings something unique to Sheffield's literary scene.

La Biblioteka
@labiblioteka

THE SOMMELIER

Barks Wine Shop is (probably) the smallest wine bar in the UK – a compact but confident space offering owner and sommelier Charles Cornelius' fresh take on fantastic wine. The weekly rotating list spans the esoteric, the affordable and the just plain delicious, with most bottles priced between £12 and £35. You can drink in or take out, and with £5 corkage (one of the lowest in Sheffield), it's a laid-back way to try something new. Regular tastings bring themed flights and collaborations with local makers. Unfussy, approachable and seriously well-stocked, Barks proves that great wine doesn't have to take itself too seriously.

Barks Wine Shop
@barks.wine

THE LANDLADY

A leading voice in Sheffield's indie beer scene, Jules Gray has built Hop Hideout into much more than a bottle shop. With seven taps, shelves of artisan cans and bottles, plus natural wines, ciders and no/low options, it's a cosy space that champions quality, independence and community. Expect small-batch breweries, female-led producers and rare imports from Germany to Belgium – plus snacks, kombucha and an ever-welcoming vibe. As founder of Sheffield Beer Week and Indie Beer Feast, Jules is a true local trailblazer, using beer to bring people together – and proving pint-sized places can have a big impact.

Hop Hideout
@hophideout

good books
& other essentials
La Biblioteka

BARKS
WINE SHOP
REALLY
NICE WINES.

MENU
LOVELY BEERS
TASTY CIDERS & PERRIES
GLORIOUS GLASSES OF WINE

ALE

THE CERAMICIST

The most recent addition to the yard is Mel Macdonald's Earth Paper Fibre – a ceramics studio, shop and workshop space bringing fresh creative energy to the courtyard. Every item on the shelves is handmade by Mel herself, crafted on-site and fired at home – a true one-woman operation rooted in passion. The studio also hosts laid-back workshops where visitors can make and decorate their own piece – from fruit plates to seasonal keepsakes – no experience needed. With monthly calendars, private bookings and a friendly, social vibe, it's about more than pottery: it's about getting stuck in, making something beautiful and having fun while you do.

Earth Paper Fibre
@earth_paper_fibre

THE CURATOR

Gravel Pit is the kind of shop you didn't know you needed to check out – until the plants in the window pull you in. Inside, it's a curated mix of botanicals, art, vinyl and homewares, packed with what owner Danny Mager calls "unnecessary necessities" – pieces that delight, spark curiosity and make a space feel like your own. Their Leah's Yard outpost (found just next to the main entrance) is a compact counterpart to the original store on Abbeydale Road, both driven by a love of music, design and good vibes. From rare plants to low-key bangers on wax, everything's chosen with care – and if you're lucky, Danny might even call you 'angel'.

Gravel Pit
@gravelpit_shop

THE ARTIST

Sheffield's beloved chronicler of everyday life, Pete McKee, brings his signature humour and heartfelt storytelling to Leah's Yard with his relocated gallery and retail space. Sitting at the opposite side of the entrance to Gravel Pit, the shop showcases a curated selection of prints, books and exclusive merchandise – all celebrating the characters, communities and culture Pete's known for. It's bold, brilliant and full of heart, just like the work itself. With rotating collections and special releases, it's a must-visit for fans old and new – and a fitting home for one of the city's most iconic creative voices.

McKee Gallery
@petemckee

We're Open!

POSTER CONVENTION & SOCIAL
OPEN HOUSE
THE REPTILES

DET
ROIT
313

CAMBRIDGE ST.
Gallery
VIVA LA NANI

REDGATES

THE FLORIST

At the heart of the yard, Roots & Bloom CIC is more than just a flower shop – founded by Gina O'Connor as a social enterprise to support people living with young onset dementia, it's rooted in purpose as much as petals. At the forefront of its mission are free monthly Gather & Grow sessions – therapeutic horticulture workshops designed to nurture creativity, calm and connection for those navigating early cognitive change. The shop itself is a haven of sustainably grown, locally sourced blooms, hand-tied arrangements and thoughtful gifts. Every purchase supports the wider mission, helping to fund its community work while customers take home flowers full of meaning. A blend of beauty, care and social impact, Roots & Bloom brings colour to both homes and lives.

Roots & Bloom
@rootsandbloomsheffield

THE CHOCOLATIER

Tucked at the back of Leah's Yard with a view over Cambridge Street Collective, Chocolate Bar is Sheffield's first café and bar dedicated entirely to cocoa – and the latest venture from award-winning bean-to-bar makers Bullion Chocolate. Founded by Max Scotford, Bullion has earned national acclaim for its luxury, ethically sourced chocolate made right here in the city. Chocolate Bar brings that same craft to a new setting, serving expertly mixed drinks, signature desserts and indulgent hot chocolates in sleek, inviting surroundings. Whether you're a connoisseur or just after something sweet, it's a refined but relaxed spot where great taste takes centre stage – morning, noon or night.

Chocolate Bar
@chocolatebaruk

THE STYLIST

Where luxury meets sustainability, Clothes the Loop brings curated designer fashion into the courtyard – and gives it a second life. Founded by sustainability expert Hellen Stirling-Baker, this stylish studio champions circular fashion over fast fashion, offering premium preloved pieces from the likes of Prada, Gucci and Stella McCartney. Carefully sourced and authenticated, every item is chosen with quality, longevity and planet-conscious shopping in mind. Think timeless coats, iconic bags and statement pieces that deserve to be loved again (and again). It's fashion with a lighter footprint – and a whole lot of style.

Clothes the Loop
@clothes_the_loop

£12
Soul Sister
Token £3.00

Filson
CHOCO LATE

CHOCO LATE

KAPITAL

A European beer hall with Sheffield soul

Kapital on Wellington Street brings a touch of European beer culture to Sheffield's city centre – a stylish new landmark for the city's independent bar scene.

Sheffield's city centre gained a serious dose of continental flair this summer with the opening of Kapital – a vast, Euro-inspired beer hall and restaurant from the team behind Abbeydale Road favourite, Two Thirds Beer Co. Located on Wellington Street within the £470 million Heart of the City development, this ambitious spot offers a fresh, grown-up take on the traditional beer hall experience.

Spread across two floors and 4,500 square feet, the venue combines striking industrial design with plenty of warm social energy. There's a mezzanine, a dedicated dining area and a wraparound outdoor beer garden perfect for whiling away the warmer days. With 33 taps pouring across both levels, Kapital now boasts one of the city's most impressive selections of European beer.

A standout feature is its exclusive unpasteurised Czech tank Pilsner, served fresh from Budějovický Budvar. The team installed four 500-litre tanks to ensure Sheffield gets thousands of crisp, brewery-fresh pints each week – a rarity in the UK and a nod to continental beer-drinking culture done properly.

The food offering mirrors that spirit, taking cues from kitchens across Europe. Expect XXL bratwurst, schnitzel specials and dark beer goulash alongside modern pub classics and Sunday roasts that put flavour and portion size first. It's comfort food with character, designed to pair perfectly with a cold pint.

Importantly, this isn't a UK-style beer hall full of clichés – there are no plastic lederhosen outfits or oompah bands in sight. Instead, it's a stylish, relaxed space that evolves throughout the day. Lunchtimes are mellow and laidback, while evenings up the ante with live DJs, house bands and plenty of glass-clinking with cheery toasts.

Built with patience and persistence, Kapital has already become a beloved part of Sheffield's independent bar scene. Drawing on European traditions while staying true to that innovative local spirit, it's a place where great beer, food and atmosphere come together to create something truly memorable.

Kapital
14 Wellington Street
S1 4HD
0114 399 4825
@kapitalsheffield
kapitalsheffield.com

Photos: Victoria Greensmith

KAPITAL
KAPITAL
KAPITAL
KAPITAL

CAMBRIDGE STREET COLLECTIVE

United flavours of Sheffield

In Sheffield's Heart of the City, Cambridge Street Collective brings global flavours together under one spectacular roof. Set in a transformed warehouse, it's a vibrant three-storey food hall where street food, music, art and atmosphere unite.

Welcome to Cambridge Street Collective – Europe's largest purpose-built food hall and a flagship destination in Sheffield's ever-evolving Heart of the City. Spread across three floors in a strikingly repurposed former warehouse, it's a bold celebration of global cuisine, communal dining and architectural flair.

With space for over 1,000 diners and a line-up of 20+ vendors, the Collective brings together a dizzying variety of flavours under one stylish roof. Whether you're craving fiery Thai stir-fries, hand-pulled Vietnamese noodles, slow-cooked Caribbean classics, Neapolitan-style pizzas or innovative plant-based eats, you'll find something to get stuck into across the hall's 20+ food stalls. With flavours spanning the globe from Malaysia to Mexico, it's a one-stop-shop for street food lovers.

The venue's design effortlessly blends the old and new: exposed brick, steel beams and heritage tiles pay homage to the building's industrial past, while sleek lighting and vibrant interiors usher in a new era for the city's dining scene. At the top, there's a rooftop terrace bar offering skyline views and cocktails late into the night.

But CSC is more than just a place to eat. With private dining spaces, regular DJ sets, live music and art installations, it's fast become a social hub – a space to gather, graze and explore. The in-house bar is expertly stocked, the coffee is locally roasted, and with everything from quick bites to full-blown feasts on offer, it's equally suited to lunch breaks, date nights or big group outings.

Much like the city it calls home, Cambridge Street Collective is full of character, flavour and independent spirit. Pull up a chair, grab a fork and dive in.

Cambridge Street Collective
32 Cambridge Street
S1 4HP
0114 3221020
@cambridge_street_collective

MICHIES
Detroit Style
Pizzeria

PALESTINIAN KITCHEN

DOG & PARTRIDGE

A Sheffield institution with an unmistakably Irish heart.

Step inside the Dog & Partridge, Sheffield's oldest continuously serving pub, where Irish warmth, award-winning pints, wholesome food and live music create a home-from-home brimming with charm and community spirit.

The Dog & Partridge is one of Sheffield's oldest pubs, still full of life and character. First recorded in 1797, it's recognised as our longest continuously serving public house – and under the care of Conor and Sarah Smith, it has grown into one of the city's most celebrated spots. Named among Guinness's Top 10 Pubs in the UK for both 2024 and 2025, and winner of Best Traditional Pub at the Exposed Magazine Awards in consecutive years, it's a true local landmark.

Conor's Irish roots and decades of experience in hospitality have shaped the way he and Sarah run the pub. For them, a good pub should feel like walking into someone's home rather than a business, and that sense of welcome – of inviting people into their space – comes through in every friendly greeting and perfectly pulled pint. It's an ethos fully shared by their team, one that turns regulars into friends and chance visitors into familiar faces.

As a free house, the pub celebrates independence in every sense. The bar boasts a rotating line-up of craft beer and local cask ales alongside the "holy trinity" of Irish stouts – Guinness, Beamish and Murphy's – poured to perfection. Whiskey lovers are well catered for too, with more than 20 Irish varieties on offer, from household names to sought-after editions.

The kitchen has earned its own loyal following. Irish-inspired dishes such as Dublin Coddle, homemade sausage rolls and the iconic Tayto sandwich are joined by the Spice Basket – their version of the Dublin takeaway favourite – and the infamous Chips o' Doom, which attracts heat enthusiasts from across the region eager to earn the coveted survivor's badge.

Music and community are at the heart of the pub. Regular trad sessions, bluegrass nights and acoustic jams sit alongside quizzes, Irish bingo, art events and charity fundraisers. The bi-monthly Dogfest brings a full day of live music from local artists, while on a weekday evening you might pop in to find book clubs gathered in the snug or food drives for the S6 Foodbank in full swing.

Inclusive, characterful and full of heart, 'the Dog' continues to embody what a real pub should be – a meeting place, a refuge and a celebration of independent spirit.

Dog & Partridge
56 Trippet Ln
S1 4EL

@dogandpartridge sheffield
thedogsheffield.com

BEAMISH
GUINNESS
BEAMISH
GUINNESS

GUINNESS

WINDSOR

NEAT PICKS

A Landlord's Guide to Irish Whiskey

Dog & Partridge is best known for its friendly atmosphere, quality beer and laid-back charm – but among whiskey drinkers, it holds another reputation. Tucked behind the bar is one of the city's most lovingly assembled collections, with everything from solid everyday sippers to rare bottles you won't find anywhere else in Sheffield.

Landlord Conor Smith has spent years curating the selection. So, we asked him to pick out five of his personal favourites and talk us through why they deserve your attention – whether you're new to Irish whiskey or already know your pot still from your single malt.

Powers Distiller's Cut

43% ABV

Made at the Midleton Distillery in County Cork, this might be considered a "standard" Irish whiskey – but for my money, it's the best standard whiskey on the market right now. It's got a bold flavour, yet remains light, so I'd describe it as a perfect summer spirit. Great for sipping neat, but I love it served as a highball – tall glass, ice, soda water. A refreshing Irish take on the gin and tonic!

Teeling Single Grain Whiskey

46% ABV

This is my favourite from the Dublin-based Teeling Distillery. Non-chill filtered to retain its flavour and character, and bottled at 46%, it's got a lovely lightness with a little spicy edge – reminds me of an American rye to a degree. As such, it really shines in cocktails like a Manhattan or an Old Fashioned.

Redbreast Single Pot Still

40% ABV

Redbreast produce this in a few different age expressions, but for me, pound for pound, it's the best whiskey in the world. That's a big shout, I know, but when you consider what you're getting for the price, nothing else compares. It's rich and oily, with deep notes of figs and raisins, and even a touch of cigar box tobacco. A cracking Christmas dram, but also perfect for sipping neat any time.

The Irishman

40% ABV

A single malt, which is still fairly rare in Ireland, though they're getting more popular. This one's from Walsh Distillery in County Carlow and it's got surprising depth of flavour, considering how light it looks in the glass. Think dark chocolate, cream, fudge – it's a wonderfully indulgent whiskey.

Midleton Very Rare

40% ABV

The jewel in the crown of the Midleton Distillery in Cork. This is their flagship whiskey and one of the finest blends you'll find anywhere – though at nearly £200 a bottle, it's definitely a treat dram. A masterfully crafted blend of the best single pot still and single grain whiskeys, it's layered with nutty, fruity notes and subtle herbal tones. It's a real dream of a drink.

REDBREAST
SINGLE POT STILL
Irish Whiskey
12
SPIRIT of DUBLIN
TEELING
WHISKEY
SINGLE GRAIN
IRISH WHISKEY
THE
IRISHMAN
SINGLE MALT
IRISH WHISKEY
12
MIDLETON
VERY RARE
VINTAGE RELEASE
IRISH WHISKEY
2023
POWERS
EST 1791
IRISH
P
WHISKEY
DISTILLER'S CUT

FAGAN'S

One pub to unite them all

Fagan's remains a true Sheffield original – part pub, part legend. Now cared for by The Fellowship of Fagan's, it keeps the Guinness flowing, the folk tunes playing and the conversation lively.

There are pubs, and then there's Fagan's – a Sheffield institution where the Guinness flows, the folk music never stops, and the stories are as thick as the smoke-stained walls of decades past. So, when beloved landlords Tom and Barbara called time in 2023 after 37 glorious years, the question wasn't just what's next – it was who could possibly take it on?

Enter The Fellowship of Fagan's – a group of nine proud Sheffielders (including Arctic Monkeys drummer Matt Helders, hospitality pros James O'Hara and James Hill, film execs from Warp, a joiner, a decorator and more) who banded together via WhatsApp to make sure the soul of the pub stayed intact. Not a chain in sight – just a determined bunch who refused to let the spirit of the place be tampered with.

And true to their word, not much has changed. The Guinness is still spot on. There's live music five nights a week. The walls are still packed with Sheffield art and the conversation still flows thick and fast. There's even still no sign of Robbie Williams (still barred, apparently).

Gone is the hot food (because, let's face it, no one could follow Tom's legendary cooking), but in its place is a pub sharpened just enough for the modern day – card machines, later opening hours, after-show parties for touring bands and even exhibitions, like a recent show by Sheffield artist Melville. It's all still unmistakably Fagan's – just with a bit of extra polish.

Tucked just off Broad Lane and forming part of Sheffield's historic Irish Triangle alongside The Grapes and Dog & Partridge, Fagan's is still a sanctuary in the city – for musicians, locals, artists and anyone in search of a proper pint and a story worth hearing.

Fagan's
69 Broad Lane
S1 4BS

@fagansheffield

All photos @Pedalo except pub exterior

FAGAN'S
AMSTEL

STEELWORKS
FAGAN'S
PUBLIC
LOUNGE

THE THREE TUNS

A Sheffield classic revived

An 18th-century Sheffield landmark brought back to life, the flat-iron pub has been lovingly restored into a warm, characterful space where good food, music and community spirit once again fill the air.

For years, The Three Tuns stood quietly on the edge of the city centre, its distinctive flat-iron shape catching the eye of passers-by but its doors all too often closed. Today, the historic pub has found new life thanks to owner Jim Butterell and his team, who have lovingly brought one of Sheffield's most recognisable buildings back into use.

Tucked between Paradise Square and Broad Lane, the 18th-century pub has long been part of the city's social history and remains one of its most striking examples of traditional architecture. Jim, a commercial interior designer by trade, has carefully restored the space, giving it warmth and personality without losing its heritage or charm.

Inside, the bow-shaped room retains its original character but feels refreshed. Sanded floors, vintage red wall panels and mid-century furniture create a relaxed, welcoming setting, while the gentle buzz of conversation and lovingly curated vinyl-only playlists give it a sense of belonging once more. Locals have embraced the gradual transformation, enjoying the feeling of being part of the pub's revival.

The Three Tuns still serves as a traditional city pub, but there's a renewed spark running through it. Supper Clubs showcase guest chefs and inventive menus, quiz nights fill the midweek calendar and creative sessions such as pottery classes and craft workshops bring something different to the table. Regulars have also fallen for the "bring your own vinyl" nights, where anyone can add their records to the evening's playlist.

Sundays are all about comfort, with generous roasts served with all the trimmings – crispy potatoes, Yorkshire puddings and a proper sticky toffee pudding to finish. It's the kind of meal that feels right at home in a place built on Sheffield tradition.

Blending history with a new sense of purpose, this quirky spot has reclaimed its place in the city's pub landscape – a true landmark reborn for both long-time regulars and new generations to enjoy.

The Three Tuns
39 Silver Street Head
S1 2DD

@thethreetuns.sheffield
www.thethreetuns.co

WORK
HARD
&
BE NICE
TO PEOPLE

THE OLD SHOE

Putting their best foot forward

A stand-out city centre hangout, The Old Shoe brings together exceptional pours, passionate staff and a laid-back atmosphere to create an award-winning Orchard Square bar

Set in a (you guessed it) former shoe shop in Orchard Square, The Old Shoe has quickly become one of Sheffield city centre's standout spots for discerning drinkers. Blending the best elements of a craft beer taproom, artisan wine bar and modern ciderhouse, it's the brainchild of Mike Pomranz and Matt Beety – a familiar duo on Sheffield's craft beer and wine scene, driven by a shared belief that great drinks deserve to be enjoyed in a welcoming, unpretentious setting.

Step inside and you'll find 26 rotating taps pouring a mix of intriguing craft beers, ciders and kegged wines, alongside an ever-evolving list of artisan wines, small-batch spirits and imaginative soft drinks. The team's own Exemption Ciderhouse produces cider made from foraged Sheffield apples, adding a hyperlocal touch to the menu. It's a venue built on discovery – where beer drinkers might find themselves converted to orange wine, or wine lovers realise they've got a taste for sours.

Service sits at the heart of The Old Shoe's success. Staff are friendly, knowledgeable and genuinely passionate about helping guests explore what's on offer, ensuring that every pour is matched by a sense of warmth and curiosity. Add to that a sleek yet inviting interior, good vinyl on the decks and a relaxed buzz from the growing Orchard Square community, and you've got a bar that feels both contemporary and comfortable.

Crowned Best New Bar at the Exposed Awards in 2024 and following it up with Best Bar in 2025, The Old Shoe shows no signs of slowing down. From creating their own in-house soft drinks to hosting tastings, collaborations and special events, the team continues to push boundaries while staying true to their ethos: serve great drinks, done properly. A hybrid haven for beer, wine and cider lovers alike, The Old Shoe is quietly redefining what a city centre bar can be.

The Old Shoe
Unit 20
Orchard Square
S1 2FB
07470 312505
@theoldshoebar

THE OLD SHOE
THE OLD SHOE
MICROCIDERY
HANDCRAFTED SOFT DRINKS
THE OLD SHOE
OPEN

THE OLD SHOE

CUBANA

25 years of rhythm, flavour and unmatchable vibes

Sheffield's home of Latin flavour, rhythm and flair. What began as a small tapas bar has become a city institution revered for its authentic dishes, live music and salsa nights.

For a quarter of a century, Cubana has brought the vibrant spirit of Latin America to Sheffield. What began life as a small but lively tapas bar on Trippet Lane in 2000 has grown into one of the city's most iconic venues – a place where food, music and dance come together in a joyful celebration of culture and community. The accolades are numerous, and its rum collection – more than 300 varieties sourced from across the globe – has been praised by world rum ambassador Ian A. V. Burrell as one of the finest anywhere.

Now firmly rooted in Leopold Square since 2014, Cubana is a vibrant mix of restaurant, cocktail bar and live music venue, famous for its infectious energy and colourful atmosphere. Together, co-owners Adrian Bagnoli and Brad Charlesworth have created something unique and lasting – a bustling social hub designed to celebrate the finer things in life.

Over the years, the venue has enjoyed plenty of unforgettable moments. It became a favourite of the legendary Buena Vista Social Club, hosting three exclusive after-parties for the 13-piece Cuban act between 2007 and 2009. The team has also welcomed Panamanian boxing icon Roberto Duran and even cooked for Aleida Guevara – daughter of revolutionary hero Che Guevara – shortly after the move to bigger premises.

The menu blends classic Spanish tapas with bold South American flavours, earning national recognition for its creativity and consistency. Diners can enjoy everything from sizzling meats and fresh seafood to inventive plant-based dishes and their famous albondigas (meatballs), all designed for sharing and paired with fine wines and expertly mixed cocktails that capture the essence of Havana nightlife.

Music has always been at the heart of Cubana. The venue hosts live performances almost every evening, featuring local talent and international acts that fill the space with rhythm and soul. Perhaps its most famous event, Salsa in the Square, transforms the square into an open-air fiesta three times a year. Hundreds gather for live bands, dance displays and a shared sense of celebration that has made it a staple of the city's cultural calendar.

After 25 years, Cubana remains a true symbol of independent spirit – a place that continues to evolve while staying true to its roots. With great food, warm hospitality and Latin passion at its core, it's no wonder Sheffield still can't stop dancing.

Cubana
4 Leopold Square
S1 2JG
0114 276 0475
cubanatapasbar.co.uk
@cubanasheffield

TABACOS

CUBAN BAR

25 YEARS OF CUBANA

How a Latin-inspired dream became a Sheffield institution – with co-owner **Adrian Bagnoli**...

Let's rewind to 2000 – how did Cubana first come about?

When promoting Latin club nights from 1995 – 1999, it was obvious there was a real love for Latin music in Sheffield. I teamed up with business partners Brad and Kito to try and create a more permanent space for this, which is when we secured the place on Trippet Lane. Alongside the music, we wanted to bring in food – Spanish tapas felt like the perfect combination!

What do you remember about those first few chaotic weeks?

They were, like you said, chaotic! We weren't actually allowed to sell alcohol for the first month, but we took this setback and chose to really focus on the food, which has become integral to Cubana ever since. It was a hectic time, but once we opened and people flooded through the doors, none of that mattered anymore – they just loved what we did.

Over 25 years, Cubana has become a real Sheffield institution. At what point did you realise it had grown into something bigger than just a restaurant or bar?

Probably when we moved to Leopold Square. It was scary because people loved our venue on Trippet Lane, but it was exciting to see what was to come. And looking back, it's been a fabulous 11 years.

You've welcomed some pretty special guests over the years. What's been the most surreal or memorable night in Cubana's history?

Che Guevara's daughter was probably as good as it gets – she was so complimentary about the food, the atmosphere, everything. Equally, when the Buena Vista Social Club came two years running, they had their after-concert party at Cubana, and some of their musicians played – that was a very special night.

What do you think makes Cubana's atmosphere so distinctive after all these years?

Cubana has that fun holiday vibe, with live upbeat music, delicious food and a friendly team that just makes people smile and de-stress as soon as they walk in.

What does this 25-year milestone mean to you both personally?

To still be here after 25 years in hospitality really means something. It comes down to hard work, and the strong bond Brad and I have built. But above all, it's the good fortune of having very many fantastic staff members work for us and being part of the Cubana family over the years. We've also seen nearly three generations of families from Sheffield enjoy Cubana, and that's really special.

RED MULLET WITH SALSA & POTATOES

This Spanish-inspired dish brings together crispy-skinned red mullet, golden baby potatoes and sweet roasted peppers. It's topped with a fresh cucumber, lime and coriander salsa for contrast and zing. A perfect light main course that's full of colour, flavour and texture – and easy to prepare in under 30 minutes.

Preparation time: 20–30 minutes | Cooking time: 8–10 minutes | Serves: 2

Ingredients

10 baby new potatoes
½ cucumber
1 small white onion
Small bunch fresh coriander
1 lime
1 red pepper
Extra virgin olive oil
2 red mullet fillets
Salt
Black pepper

Method

Boil the potatoes in salted water until just tender, then set aside.

Meanwhile, peel and deseed the cucumber. Boil briefly, then chop and place in a bowl.

Finely dice the onion and chop the coriander. Add both to the cucumber and squeeze in lime juice to taste – this is your salsa.

Chop the red pepper and cook in a hot cast iron pan with a little oil until softened and slightly charred.

Add a splash more oil to the pan and place the red mullet skin-side down. Add the cooked potatoes and roasted peppers around the fish.

After about 3 minutes, turn the fish over. Transfer the pan to a hot oven (190°C) and roast for 5 minutes until the fish is cooked through.

Season with salt, pepper and another squeeze of lime juice.

To serve

Plate up the potatoes and peppers, top with the fish, then spoon over the cucumber salsa to finish. Serve immediately.

Cubana
4 Leopold Square
S1 2JG
0114 276 0475
cubanatapasbar.co.uk
@cubanasheffield

EL PRESIDENTE COCKTAIL

A Havana-born classic with true old-school glamour, El Presidente first appeared in the 1910s and has been a classic ever since. At Cubana, the version served today blends the best elements from past recipes – and showcases the elegant Havana Club Selección de Maestros in a drink that's smooth, complex and deeply satisfying.

Preparation time: 5 minutes | Serves: 1

Ingredients

50ml Havana Club Selección de Maestros
25ml Cocchi Americano
5ml Cocchi Vermouth di Torino
10ml Ferrand Dry Curaçao
2.5ml grenadine

Method

Add all ingredients to a mixing glass filled with ice.
Stir well until chilled – about 30 seconds.
Strain into a chilled cocktail glass.

To serve

Garnish with an orange twist if desired. Best served straight up, no ice, to let the flavours shine.

Cubana
4 Leopold Square
S1 2JG
0114 276 0475
cubanatapasbar.co.uk
@cubanasheffield

GRAN AÑEJO
ICONICA
Havana Club
SELECCIÓN DE
MAESTROS
FROM HAND-SELECTED
RESERVE CASKS
RON
GRAN AÑEJO

CHINA RED

Tongue-tingling tastes on The Moor

A celebrated Sheffield spot serving authentic Sichuan dishes, China Red has two decades of experience offering everything from group feasts to full-blown karaoke nights.

In a city brimming with global cuisine, China Red brings something truly distinctive to the table: bold, flavour-packed Sichuan food made by chefs who know it best. Found just off The Moor, this proudly independent restaurant has been flying the flag for authentic Sichuan cooking in Sheffield since 2006.

Step inside and you'll find a vibrant, welcoming space designed for social dining – the kind that's made for sharing. Tables are fitted with traditional Lazy Susans to encourage a communal approach, turning mealtimes into experiences. It's a popular spot for family gatherings, parties and celebrations, and now even offers outside catering and buffet services for events and corporate functions.

Upstairs, a fully kitted-out karaoke bar adds another layer to the fun – making China Red not just a place to eat, but to enjoy a proper night out.

The kitchen is led by a passionate team of chefs trained in Sichuan province, the birthplace of this bold cuisine. Here, spice is all about balance – flavour, aroma, and that famous tingling sensation from Sichuan peppercorns. The menu mixes crowd-pleasers with more adventurous plates, from fragrant cumin lamb to bubbling hot pots.

Everything is cooked fresh to order, with house-made staples like pickled vegetables and chilli oil bringing extra depth to the dishes. It's also a vegan-friendly menu, with plenty of plant-based options that don't compromise on authenticity or taste.

Crowned Best Sichuan Restaurant in the UK at the Golden Panda Awards, China Red is as celebrated as it is consistent. A lively, flavourful tribute to one of China's most exciting regional cuisines – right in the heart of Sheffield.

China Red
3 Rockingham Gate
S1 4JD
0114 272 1332

@chinaredsheffield

YUXIANG AUBERGINE

Yuxiang is a famous seasoning mixture in Chinese cuisine which originated from Sichuan province. Despite the term meaning 'fish fragrance' in Chinese, it contains no fish or seafood.

Preparation time: 15 minutes | Cooking time: 10 minutes | Serves: 2

Yuxiang aubergine is a symbolic Sichuan dish in Chinese cuisine which is salty, sour, sweet, spicy and fragrant, and loaded with the holy trinity of spring onion, ginger and garlic.

Ingredients:

2 aubergines
1 ½tsp salt
2½ tsp cornstarch
3 tbsp vegetable oil
4 tsp minced garlic
4 tsp minced fresh ginger
2 red chillies, finely chopped
2 tbsp Sichuan chilli bean paste (doubanjiang)
3 tbsp Henderson's Relish
2 tbsp Shaoxing wine (or dry sherry)
1 tbsp white sugar
2 tsp soy sauce
4 spring onions, cut into 1cm pieces
Fresh coriander, roughly chopped

Method:

Trim the aubergines, split them into quarters lengthwise and cut into 8 – 10cm lengths, then place in a big bowl. Add the salt, cover with water, then leave to soak for 15 minutes. Squeeze the water out of the aubergine with your hands, place it on a plate and sprinkle the cornstarch all over the aubergine, making sure each piece is fully coated.

Next, heat the oil in a wok until smoking. Reduce the heat to medium and add the aubergine, stir frying until the aubergine becomes softened and golden brown on all sides, which should take about 5 minutes. Remove the aubergine from the wok and put it aside.

Using the same wok over a high heat, add the minced garlic, ginger and chopped chilli. Stir until they become fragrant and any raw bite is gone. Add the chilli bean paste to the wok and stir-fry for about 30 seconds until fragrant. Put the aubergine back into the wok along with the Henderson's Relish, Shaoxing wine, white sugar, and soy sauce. Stir and toss the mixture constantly for about 3 minutes until the sauce is thick, glossy and coats the aubergine nicely.

Finally, add the spring onions to the wok, mix well and fry for 30 seconds. Turn off the heat, transfer the cooked aubergine to a serving plate, garnish with the fresh coriander and serve immediately with steamed jasmine rice.

China Red
3 Rockingham Gate
S1 4JD
0114 272 1332
@chinaredsheffield

ORCHARD SQUARE

Where Sheffield life comes into full bloom

Whether you're heading for a bite, browsing the shops or catching up over drinks, there's always something going on at Orchard Square, making it a natural meeting point for socialising in the heart of town.

A lively open-air hub in the heart of Sheffield, Orchard Square brings together shopping, dining and entertainment in one welcoming space. Following a major refurbishment in 2023 - complete with a canopy-covered terrace and outdoor seating - the square has become a go-to destination for locals and visitors to meet, eat, drink and unwind.

Home to an eclectic mix of independent retailers and well-known high street names, Orchard Square reflects the city's creative, community-driven spirit. Visitors can browse boutiques alongside brands like TK Maxx and Waterstones, discovering everything from fashion and homeware to gifts and accessories. The regular Makers' Markets add to the appeal, filling the space with local crafts, handmade goods and Sheffield-made treasures.

Food and drink take centre stage here too. The Square's dining line-up ranges from Proove's award-winning Neapolitan pizzas to the bold Punjabi and North Indian flavours of Chatori Gali by 5Tara. The Old Shoe, a craft beer, wine and cider bar, offers one of the most diverse drinks selections in the UK, served in relaxed, sociable surroundings.

Visitors love the space and views from the terrace venues too... which include cocktail bar and home of O.G. Detroit Pizza, Terrace Goods as well as their dive bar neighbour, Cheap Dates.

At the heart of it all sits Sheffield Plate, a bustling food hall showcasing global street food and local talent under one roof. From daytime dining to late-night bites, it's a spot made for sharing meals and moments. Regular live music, family activities and community events give the venue its friendly, inclusive energy, making it much more than a place to grab lunch.

Entertainment also plays its part. Game Show All-Stars, created by the team behind Sheffield's Great Escape Rooms, brings a playful edge to proceedings, letting visitors step into their favourite TV games for a dose of light-hearted competition.

Together, these elements make Orchard Square a microcosm of Sheffield life; creative, independent and full of character. Whether you're shopping, socialising, eating or exploring, it's a vibrant, ever-evolving space that celebrates the best of the city's culture and community.

Orchard Square
41 Orchard Street
S1 2FB

@orchardsquare
orchardsquare.co.uk

CHEAP
DATES

FOOD
HALL

PHOTOBOOTH
CHEAP
DATES

WOKIE BOX

Wok this way

Bringing wok-fired energy to Furnival Gate, Wokie Box serves fast, fresh Asian-inspired dishes made to order. From noodles and rice boxes to crispy sides and bold sauces, it's quick, customisable and full of flavour.

Wokie Box brings big flavour and wok-fired flair to Furnival Gate, offering a fresh spin on fast food inspired by Chinese, Japanese, Korean and Malaysian cuisines, with a menu that's fully customisable and packed with punch. The younger sibling to long-standing Szechuan favourite China Red, it's a casual concept with serious flavour credentials.

Here, food is cooked to order at blistering heat, delivering quick-turnaround dishes that don't compromise on taste. You choose your base (noodles or rice), pick your protein, veg and sauce, and watch as it's stir-fried to perfection in a matter of minutes. If choice paralysis strikes, the curated Special Boxes have your back – think sticky sweet and sour chicken or aromatic Singapore vermicelli, all from around £9 a box.

Sides are just as tempting, with golden spring rolls, crispy wontons and salt-and-pepper chips offering classic comfort, while the zingy dipping sauces add that signature Wokie twist. The whole menu is rooted in authentic Asian flavours, but made accessible, affordable and fast – ideal for busy city lunches, post-shop pit stops or late-night feasting.

Despite the street food-style packaging, Wokie Box doesn't cut corners on quality. Ingredients are fresh, sauces are punchy, and everything is cooked with the same care and attention that defines its big sister, China Red. There's even space to eat in, with a comfy dining area just steps from the action of the open kitchen – a perfect spot to catch the flames and soak up the buzz.

Whether you're craving a quick bite, curating your dream combo or working your way through the specials, Wokie Box delivers bold, balanced fast food that hits the spot every time. Quick, tasty and totally satisfying – this is East Asian street food done the Sheffield way.

Wokie Box
26 Furnival Gate
S1 4QP
0114 296 2620
@wokiebox

GUYSHI

Where cooking meets connection

A striking West Street destination where Japanese charcoal grilling, tableside cooking and inventive drinks come together under moody lighting and a standout Sakura centrepiece.

Bringing Japanese charcoal BBQ dining to West Street with serious flair, Guyshi combines traditional yakiniku with a sleek, modern setting.

This is food as experience – where sizzling cuts are cooked by diners over smokeless yakiniku grills built into each table. Expect conversation, flames and flavour in equal measure

The yakiniku menu features premium meats, seafood and vegetables – from garlic pork ribs and cheesy garlic scallops to king prawns and melt-in-the-mouth A5 wagyu. Vegan diners are well catered for too, with sushi rolls and mock-meat platters holding their own against the carnivorous options. Fresh sashimi, kushiyaki skewers and donburi bowls round out the offering, alongside DIY s'mores for the sweet-toothed and an all-you-can-eat Utage menu for the indecisive or the hungry, inviting you to taste your way through it all.

For something a bit different, the intimate teppanyaki experience brings a dedicated chef to your table, where you'll get front-row seats to sizzling plates, knife-twirling tricks and flame-roaring entertainment that turn dinner into theatre.

Behind the bar, the same spirit of craftsmanship shines through. Sake flows from a traditional cooling tower, poured with ceremony and precision. The cocktail menu blends Japanese creativity with flair – think yuzu spritzes, matcha martinis, sakura sours and playful twists on the classics. There's also a thoughtful selection of Japanese whiskies and beers, plus a wine list curated to complement the umami-rich flavours. It's the kind of bar where you can pull up a stool and linger long after your last bite, exploring the drinks as deeply as the food.

Guyshi's interiors are every bit as memorable as its menu. The space feels luxurious yet approachable – rich marble surfaces, low lighting and plush seating gathered beneath a large Sakura tree anchoring the space, with a sweeping marble staircase leading the way. All watched over by Yuki, the restaurant's charming yet sassy robot cat, who glides between tables to deliver dishes and serenades guests on their birthdays.

There's an energy at Guyshi that's hard to bottle – a place where time seems to slow as the glow of the coals meets the hum of conversation and the pulse of the city outside. It's dining as connection: designed to bring people together and leave a lasting impression.

Guyshi
180 West Street
S1 4ET

@guyshi_sheffield
www.guyshi.co.uk

FREE DRINK

KIRIN

JOOMAK

Seoul food

Bringing the spirit of Seoul to Furnival Gate, Joomak is a vibrant Korean kitchen and bar serving bold, shareable dishes and late-night energy.

Part Korean kitchen, part bar, Joomak blends traditional flavours with modern flair – and it's fast becoming one of the city's best-kept dining secrets.

Taking its name from Korea's casual drinking dens, Joomak brings the spirit of Seoul to Furnival Gate, delivering comfort food classics, K-pop playlists and an unmistakable sense of fun. The space itself is vibrant, with bold orange seating, neon wall art, and retro grabber toy machines that give the place its playful, late-night energy.

At the heart of it all is the food. Everything is cooked fresh to order, bursting with flavour and perfect for sharing. The Korean Fried Chicken – crisp, glazed and addictive – is a runaway customer favourite, served alongside bulgogi beef, kimchi pancakes, steaming hot pots and house-made pickles. Generous portions and punchy flavours are the name of the game, and there are plenty of vegan-friendly options to keep everyone happy.

Joomak thrives on a sociable, shared style of eating, where tables fill with dishes and chopsticks fly. It's a true reflection of the Joomak spirit – relaxed, boisterous and full of laughter. Late-night openings and a drinks list stacked with Korean soju, beer and cocktails make it a go-to for after-hours bites and casual hangs.

Beyond the dine-in experience, Joomak also offers outside catering and packed lunches for events or corporate clients – making it as flexible as it is flavourful.

From street-style dishes to a city-centre setting packed with personality, Joomak is one of those places that turns first-timers into regulars. It's unpretentious, energetic and totally delicious – a celebration of Korean food culture, right here in the middle of Sheffield.

Joomak
32 – 34 Furnival Gate
S1 4QP
0114 698 7110
@joomak.uk

JOO & MAK
KOREAN KITCHEN & PUB
JOO & MAK
KOREAN KITCHEN & PUB
TOY WORLD

BUILDER'S BREW

Everything is awesome!

Bringing a welcome splash of playfulness to the city centre, Builder's Brew has quickly become a go-to hangout for Sheffielders of all ages.

Found opposite Sheffield Cathedral, this family-run spot invites visitors to unwind, get creative and rediscover the joy of building – one brick (and one brew) at a time.

The concept is as simple as it is inspired. For a set hourly rate, guests can choose from hundreds of LEGO sets, from Star Wars and Harry Potter to intricate cityscapes and architecture builds, or dive into thousands of loose bricks for freestyle creations. By scanning the QR codes on the tables or checking the two in-house screens, visitors can browse the available sets – helpfully split by size and difficulty – making it easy to find their perfect build. Whether you're six or sixty, there's something wonderfully satisfying about switching off, stacking bricks and watching something take shape.

Run by husband-and-wife team James and Laura Beech, the idea was born out of their shared love of LEGO and family time with their six young children. What began as a dream to create a fun, family-friendly venue has quickly evolved into a buzzing social space where creativity and calm go hand in hand. Roughly half of the weekend crowd are adults — students on chilled evenings out, couples on quirky date nights, and groups of friends looking for something different.

The café's relaxed atmosphere is supported by a comforting food and drink offer with cakes, bakes and toasties made in-house, plus fresh coffee from Sheffield's Forge Coffee Roasters to keep builders fuelled.

With an upstairs space available for parties, team away days and private events, Builder's Brew continues to grow while staying rooted in its simple mission: to create a fun, affordable and creative space for everyone.

Builder's Brew
2-3 East Parade
S1 2ET

@buildersbrewcafe
buildersbrewcafe.com

shire Tea 2.90
Fruit Tea 3.20
Espresso 2.90
Americano 3.20
Flat White 3.70
Latte 3.70
Iced Latte 3.90
Cappuccino 3.70
Syrups 50
Hot Chocolate 3.70
Mocha 3.90
Cans 2.50
Juice 2.50
Fruit Shoot 1.80
Yazoo 2.50
Water 1.50
BUILDER'S CREW

BUILDER'S BREW

FRAZER'S COFFEE ROASTERS

Proper coffee, done the Sheffield way

Frazer's Coffee Roasters has grown from a homemade barbecue roaster to an award-winning Sheffield institution, roasting every batch on-site and staying true to its roots of craft, community and authenticity.

Walk into Frazer's Coffee Roasters on Arundel Street and the first thing you'll notice isn't just the smell of freshly roasted beans, but the hum of a friendly working space built on graft. Every roast, blend and brew is handled on-site by founder Frazer Habershon and his team, in a building woven into the history of the neighbourhood.

The café and roastery sit inside a former 19th-century coach repair house, its old Sheffield-made bricks still visible throughout. Frazer restored and repurposed the space himself, keeping its raw, industrial charm intact while turning it into a welcoming hub for coffee lovers. The open layout means visitors can see and hear the roasting in action – a transparent approach that mirrors the brand's down-to-earth ethos.

The story began in 2014 with a homemade barbecue roaster – built using discarded Forgemasters steel – and a clear aim to make artisan coffee without the pretence. From those DIY beginnings to the thriving spot it is today, the focus has stayed on quality, community and doing things the right way. Every batch is still roasted on the same hand-built machine that started it all, with beans sourced directly from farmers Frazer knows personally. This direct trade approach builds lasting relationships across the globe, supports fair practice and keeps the story behind each bean at the heart of the cup.

That commitment has taken the brand far beyond its roots. Frazer's now supplies major organisations including WHSmith, HSBC and Facebook, alongside countless local cafés, bars and customers who buy direct. The business's newest addition, a drive-through in Ecclesfield, makes its coffee even more accessible while keeping the same independent spirit.

The quality hasn't gone unnoticed. Frazer's has picked up multiple Great Taste Awards – a sign of how much care goes into every roast. Closer to home, it's twice taken home the "Made in Sheffield" title at the Exposed Awards – a local nod that Frazer calls a particular point of pride.

Inside the Arundel Street space, the atmosphere feels authentic and deliberately unpolished – handmade furniture, stacked sacks of beans and a trusty roaster working five days a week. It's a place that wears its craft proudly and never forgets where it came from. Like its owner, this thriving independent brand is Sheffield through and through.

Frazer's Coffee Roasters
203 Arundel Street
S1 4RE
0114 550 4000

frazerscoffee.co.uk
@frazerscoffeeroasters

CO

FRAZER'S PERFECT CAFETIÈRE BREW

There's no faff here – just good coffee, brewed the proper way. Frazer's Coffee has perfected the cafetière method so you can get the best out of your beans at home. Follow this simple guide to brew bold, balanced coffee every time – no gadgets or gimmicks, just great flavour.

Preparation time: 10 minutes | Serves: Makes up to 1 litre of coffee

Ingredients

70g freshly ground coffee per 1 litre water

Water, heated to appropriate temperature (see method)

Equipment

Cafetière (French press)
Digital scale
Kettle
Timer
Spoon or paddle

Method

Preheat the cafetière

Pour hot water into the empty cafetière and mugs to warm them. Swirl gently, leave for a minute or two, then discard the water.

Weigh and grind the coffee

Use 70g of coffee per 1 litre of water. For example, a 200ml cafetière would need 14g of coffee, and a 500ml cafetière needs 35g. Grind the beans until they resemble coarse sea salt – fresh is best.

Measure and heat the water

Weigh your water to match your ratio. Heat it according to the roast:

Light roast: 96°C

Medium roast: 94°C

Dark roast: 92°C

Don't boil – the water should be hot, but not rolling.

Add the coffee

Put the ground coffee into your preheated cafetière.

Pour and start timing

Pour the hot water evenly over the coffee. Start your timer straight away.

Stir and steep

Stir gently to ensure all grounds are saturated. Place the lid on with the plunger pulled up. Steep for 5–7 minutes, adjusting to taste.

Plunge and serve

Press the plunger down slowly and evenly. Serve the coffee immediately to avoid over-extraction.

Notes

Best enjoyed fresh. Adjust the coffee-to-water ratio slightly if you prefer a stronger or lighter brew. Always weigh your ingredients for consistency.

Frazer's Coffee Roasters
203 Arundel Street
S1 4RE
0114 550 4000
frazerscoffee.co.uk
@frazerscoffeeroasters

LOCKSLEY DISTILLING

Craft, collaboration and plenty of spirit

Founded in 2013 by husband-and-wife team John Cherry and Cynthia King, Locksley Distilling was born from a desire to make exceptional spirits rooted in authenticity and craft.

Working from a Grade II listed space at Portland Works – one of the birthplaces of Sheffield's manufacturing heritage – the distillery embodies a distinctly independent ethos, combining respect for tradition with an eye for innovation.

Locksley first made its mark with *Sir Robin of Locksley*, a gin inspired by the folklore of Loxley and one of the first off-dry gins on the market. From there, the range grew to include *Very Special Old Tom* (a navy-strength Old Tom gin) and a raspberry and cardamom edition, alongside a series of liqueurs including *Morocello* – a blood orange take on limoncello – and award-winning chocolate and coffee liqueurs made in collaboration with fellow Sheffield independents Bullion Chocolate and Foundry Coffee Roasters.

Part of what makes Locksley special is its collaborative spirit. The distillery's *Co-Lab* range brings together producers, chefs and creators who share a focus on quality, provenance, authenticity, sustainability and community.

Each partnership results in something genuinely unique – from an oyster shell-infused Amaro with Bench to a Heather and Bilberry gin celebrating the Crucible Theatre's 50th anniversary. Every project adds to an ever-expanding flavour library of more than 300 botanicals, reflecting an approach that's as inventive as it is precise.

Alongside its own spirits, Locksley also undertakes bespoke contract work for other independent brands, always maintaining the same hands-on integrity. Every bottle is distilled, labelled and finished on site, keeping the process transparent and true to its roots.

Visitors can experience this craft first-hand through the distillery's growing programme of masterclasses and tasting events. Guests are invited to tour the working distillery, learn about botanicals and flavour pairing, and create their own bespoke gin to take home – an experience that has become one of the city's most popular immersive food and drink activities.

More than a decade on, Locksley Distilling continues to evolve without losing sight of its founding principles: to make spirits with character, care and a distinctly Sheffield sense of pride.

Locksley Distilling
Portland Works
S2 4SJ

locksleydistilling.com
@locksleydistilling

VSOT
57.5%VOL
VSOT
MOROCELLO

SIR ROBIN OF LOCKSLEY
GIN

LOCKSLEY
DISTILLING Co
#leGINdary
EAT SLEEP
GIN
REPEAT

SHEFFIELD CATHEDRAL

A city landmark with a warm welcome

Sheffield Cathedral is both a historic landmark and a living community space. Inside, 1554 Coffee Shop offers local coffee, homemade cakes and friendly service – a calm retreat that reflects the Cathedral's enduring spirit of openness and connection.

Standing tall in the heart of the city centre, Sheffield Cathedral is one of its oldest and most enduring landmarks. Parts of the building date back to the 12th century, with every addition over the centuries reflecting a moment in the city's changing story. It remains a place of worship, but also a space that belongs to everyone – a civic hub, cultural venue and peaceful retreat amid the bustle of town.

Inside, visitors find 1554 Coffee Shop and 1554 Gift Shop, a welcoming spot that marks its tenth anniversary this year. The café takes its name from the year Queen Mary Tudor restored key funds to the people of Sheffield, creating a lasting link between the city and its church. Today, that same spirit of community continues.

The café is known for its friendly atmosphere and calm, light-filled space, where locals meet for lunch, tourists take a break from sightseeing and office workers drop by for coffee. Heavenly Coffee Co supplies its bespoke Cathedral blend, while cakes and bakes come from local favourites such as The Secret Cake Club and Bakewell Bakery. Vegetarian, vegan and gluten-free options are always available, and dogs are welcome too – part of the Cathedral's open-door ethos.

Next door, the gift shop showcases Sheffield's creativity, stocking work by local makers alongside regional produce and souvenirs. Its shelves feature everything from handmade gifts and Sheffield honey to exclusive Cathedral merchandise and seasonal collections, including a festive collaboration with artist Pete McKee.

Beyond worship, the Cathedral hosts a lively calendar of events. Live music events, exhibitions, festivals, film screenings and a wide range of community gatherings fill the year, alongside popular family activities and the annual Christmas Tree Festival. Together, they help the building remain what it has always been – a place for everyone in Sheffield to use, enjoy and feel part of.

Sheffield Cathedral, 1554 Coffee Shop and 1554 Gift Shop
Church Street
S1 1HA
0114 275 3434

sheffieldcathedral.org
@sheffieldcathedral

PURE RAW HONEY
THE
SHEFFIELD
HONEY
COMPANY

SHEFFIELD THEATRES

Taking centre stage

Home to the Crucible, Lyceum, Tanya Moiseiwitsch Playhouse and The Montgomery, Sheffield Theatres is the creative heart of the city. From world premieres to West End hits, it's where stories, talent and community take centre stage.

No guide to Sheffield would be complete without a mention for Sheffield Theatres. From the roar of the crowd at the Crucible to the hush before curtain-up at the Lyceum, Sheffield Theatres is the beating heart of the city's cultural life – a powerhouse of performance that's earned its stripes on the national stage and then some.

As the largest theatre complex outside of London, Sheffield Theatres is home to not one, but four world-class venues: the iconic Crucible, the grand Lyceum, the intimate Tanya Moiseiwitsch Playhouse and the latest addition, The Montgomery – form the largest theatre complex outside of London. Together, they host everything from big-name musicals and classic dramas to cutting-edge new writing and boundary-pushing experimental works.

It's the kind of place where anything feels possible – and, more often than not, it is. We're talking about the birthplace of *Everybody's Talking About Jamie*, which went from a local story to a global smash hit. Or *Standing at the Sky's Edge*, a love letter to Park Hill that picked up multiple Olivier Awards before heading back home to standing ovations. And of course, there's the small matter of the Crucible hosting the World Snooker Championship every spring – a fixture that sees Sheffield beam into living rooms around the world.

Under the leadership of artistic director Elizabeth Newman, there's a fresh energy rippling through the theatres. Her commitment to accessibility, storytelling and Sheffield's creative future is tangible – with new talent development, community programming and inclusive casting becoming central to the city's arts ecosystem.

But for all its accolades, Sheffield Theatres never feels out of reach. It's still your local – the place you go for a Saturday matinee, a midweek play or a panto with the kids. It's a space for bold ideas, big feelings and brilliant nights out. Curtain up, lights down – let's go.

Crucible Theatre and Tanya Moiseiwitsch Playhouse and Lyceum Theatre
55 Norfolk Street
S1 1DA
The Montgomery
27 Surrey Street
S1 2LG
Sheffield Theatres
0114 249 6000

@sheffieldtheatres
sheffieldtheatres.co.uk

Photos: Becky Payne except
Theatre interior: James Stewart

SHEFFIELD THEATRES
CRUCIBLE

SHEFFIELD THEATRES

SHEFFIELD MUSEUMS

Sheffield on show

Across six unique sites, Sheffield Museums celebrates the city's creativity, industry and imagination. From the Millennium Gallery's contemporary exhibitions to Kelham Island's roaring engines and Weston Park's natural history, it's a journey through Sheffield's past, present and future – where every visit tells part of the story.

From ancient tools to contemporary art, industrial grit to natural history, Sheffield Museums invites you to explore the stories that have shaped the Steel City – and continue to inspire its future. Spanning six distinct sites across the city, the group celebrates creativity, curiosity and culture in all its forms.

Start at the heart of town with the Millennium Gallery – a sleek, modern space known for bringing world-class exhibitions to Sheffield while championing local talent. Just upstairs, Graves Gallery is a quiet treasure trove of historic and contemporary artworks, housing the city's civic art collection above the buzz of the Central Library.

Up the road at Weston Park Museum, you'll find a family-friendly mix of natural history, archaeology and community stories in an elegant Victorian setting. Head south and step back in time at Abbeydale Industrial Hamlet – a lovingly preserved scythe-making works that tells the tale of Sheffield's steelmaking roots. Likewise, at the charming Shepherd Wheel Workshop in the leafy Porter Valley, a 16th-century water-powered grinding workshop has been brought back to life.

Over in Kelham Island, the museum at the area's industrial core serves as a bold reminder of Sheffield's global impact. With working engines, interactive displays and a real sense of scale, Kelham Island Museum brings the city's manufacturing past into vivid, clanking focus.

Together, Sheffield Museums manages over a million objects – from metalwork masterpieces and archaeological finds to social history artefacts and artworks – making it one of the UK's largest museum trusts outside London. But more than just preserving the past, the organisation looks to the future too, hosting inclusive events, community programmes and contemporary exhibitions that reflect Sheffield today.

Whether you're popping in for an afternoon or plotting a culture-filled weekend, Sheffield Museums offers a journey through the city's history – and into its future.

Sheffield Museums

@sheffmuseums
sheffieldmuseums.org.uk

Millenium Gallery, 48 Arundel Gate, Sheffield, S1 2PP | **Graves Gallery**, Surrey St, Sheffield, S1 1XZ | **Weston Park Museum**, Western Bank, Mushroom Lane, S10 2TP | **Abbeydale Industrial Hamlet**, Abbeydale Rd South, Beauchief, S7 2QW | **Shepherd Wheel Workshop**, Hangingwater Rd, S11 2YE | **Kelham Island Museum**, Alma St, S3 8RY

Kelham Island Museum image: Ian Spooner

KELHAM
ISLAND
MUSEUM

Millennium Gallery
MILLENNIUM GALLERY
COLOUR
Explore a World of Wonder
Free Exhibition | Please Donate £5
19 June – 14 Sep 2025
Art Fund
MILLENNIUM GALLERY
Bringing the bes
in art and design
to Sheffield
Exhibitions | Events
Shopping | Cafe

THE GREAT ESCAPE GAME

Sheffield's original adventure awaits

Sheffield's original escape room experience, The Great Escape Game mixes immersive storytelling with thrilling puzzles for a one-of-a-kind city-centre adventure.

There's something quietly legendary about The Great Escape Game. It's not just another escape room – it's one of the city's most immersive and imaginative experiences, the kind of place people talk about long after they've made their getaway. Tucked just outside the city centre, this locally grown brand has become a cornerstone of Sheffield's entertainment scene, blending clever storytelling, cinematic design and pure adrenaline into every adventure.

From the outside, you might not realise how vast the world inside is. Step through the door and you're greeted by a team who are part game master, part performer – the kind of hosts who make you forget you're playing a game at all. Each room feels like its own little universe: one moment you're locked in a detective's office, the next you're unravelling a supernatural mystery or sneaking through a criminal underworld. The set design is astonishingly detailed, the puzzles sharp and satisfying, and the pressure deliciously real as the clock ticks down.

The Great Escape Game isn't just about escape rooms either. Their Sheffield site features a bar and lounge area – the perfect pre-or post-game pitstop for celebrating triumphs or laughing about the team's spectacular near-misses. And with new games regularly added and renovated, there's always a reason to return.

Their sister site in Leeds has its own loyal following, but it's Sheffield where it all began – where the company honed its craft and helped shape the escape room scene across the UK. What started as a local idea has grown into a regional favourite, known for pushing boundaries and reimagining what immersive entertainment can be.

Whether you're a puzzle lover, thrill-seeker or just after a night that's a little different, The Great Escape Game is more than a challenge – it's an experience you'll want to get lost in.

The Great Escape Game
St. James House
Vicar Lane
S1 2EX
0330 088 3032
@thegreatescapegame
thegreatescapegame.co.uk

Images courtesy of The Great Escape Game

CAUTION

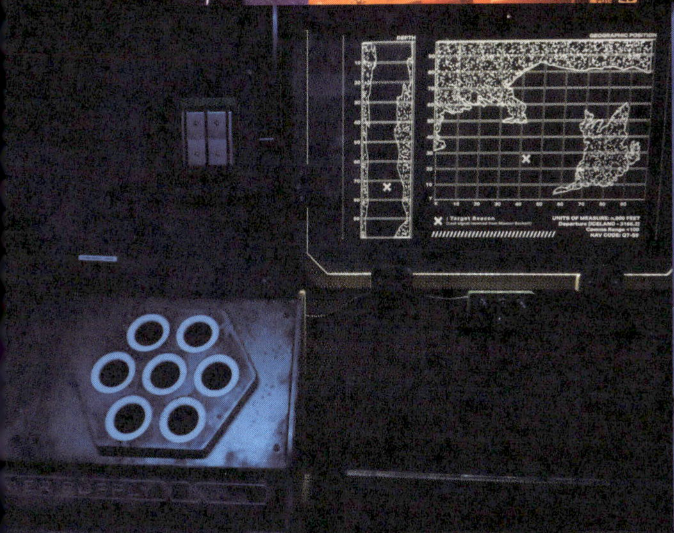
DEPTH
GEOGRAPHIC POSITION

GAMESHOW ALL-STARS

Where you're the star of the show

Step into the spotlight at Gameshow All-Stars, where classic TV game shows come to life for a buzzer bashing, high energy night out that makes you the star.

If you've ever shouted answers at the TV during Family Fortunes, debated who'd crush it on The Cube or dreamed of spinning the wheel on Wheel of Fortune, Gameshow All-Stars might just be your new obsession. Nestled in the heart of Sheffield, this one-of-a-kind activity bar brings the magic of television game shows to life – only this time, you and your friends are the contestants.

From the moment you walk through the doors, it feels like stepping onto a live TV set – bright lights, bold colours and the unmistakable buzz of friendly competition. Each game zone is modelled after iconic TV challenges, complete with real buzzers, spotlights, and a charismatic host to keep the energy high. Whether you're solving puzzles, racing against the clock, or trying to keep your cool under pressure, every moment feels like you're on set at your own prime-time show.

But it isn't just about the games. This is a full evening out – with a well-stocked bar, creative cocktails and a team that knows how to keep the good vibes flowing. Groups head down for birthdays, work nights out and just-because weekends, and it's easy to see why. It's the kind of place that gets everyone laughing, shouting, and high-fiving – even people who swore they were "just watching."

What makes it special is the balance between nostalgia and novelty. You recognise the format, but you've never experienced it quite like this – immersive, hilarious, and unashamedly fun. Gameshow All-Stars has taken the spirit of Britain's favourite pastime – the TV gameshow – and turned it into something you can actually live.

If you're after a night out that's part bar, part competition and 100% unforgettable, you'll find it here. At Gameshow All-Stars, everyone's got their moment in the spotlight.

Gameshow All-Stars
7 Orchard Square
Leopold Street
S1 2FB
0330 057 7017
@gameshowallstars
gameshowallstars.co.uk

Images courtesy of Gameshow All-Stars

THIS WAY
PHOTO BOOT

WINNER'S WHEEL
300
100
1000

PLINK PLONK

BUZZER BEATER
2200
GREEN BUZZERS ARE GREAT

SPECIAL COCKTAILS
HOLLYWOOD
PRODUCTION GAME SHOW
DIRECTOR ALL-STARS
CAMERA
DATE SCENE TAKE

THE LITTLE BOOK OF
SHEFFIELD 2025

ECCLESALL ROAD & SHARROW VALE

Heading southwest from the city centre, we land in Ecclesall Road and Sharrow Vale – two of Sheffield's most well-trodden neighbourhoods where leafy streets, buzzing independents and long-standing landmarks sit side by side.

Ecclesall Road – or Eccy Road, as it's almost universally known – is one of the city's most iconic stretches. Once a turnpike route in the early 1800s, it became a main artery for city life as Sheffield expanded westward. Grand houses and green spaces gave way to rows of shops, bars, restaurants and local businesses, earning it the nickname "The Golden Mile". Today, that same spirit remains – a lively mix of student spots, brunch places, boutiques and cocktail haunts that keep the street buzzing day and night.

It's also home to some of the city's most beautiful landmarks. On one side, the stunning Botanical Gardens – 19 acres of Victorian glasshouses, rare plants and quiet paths, and just down the slope on the other, the historic General Cemetery – the final resting place of some of Sheffield's most influential figures and a surprisingly peaceful escape from the bustle above.

Just a block over, Sharrow Vale Road offers a slower pace but no less charm. Originally farmland, the area grew into a neighbourhood of mill workers and artisans, powered by the Porter Brook. These days it's a haven for independents – from fresh fish at JH Mann and burritos at Street Food Chef, to all manner of indies in Dyson Place, hand-poured candles, jewellery and refill shops elsewhere, it's claim to be Sheffield's best indie high street is strong.

The two areas together are a proper double act. Ecclesall Road brings the energy, Sharrow Vale brings the passion – and between them, they show off some of the best of what Sheffield's local scene has to offer. Whether you're hunting down a gift for a loved one, on a big night out, planning a lazy lunch, or just wandering with a flat white in hand, there's plenty to keep you here.

So, let's keep heading southwest and meet some of the people and places that give Eccy Road and Sharrow Vale their unmistakable character...

Ashoka photo: Ellie Grace Photography, Famous
Sheffield Shop: Pete Hill

...A LIVELY MIX OF STUDENT SPOTS, BRUNCH PLACES, BOUTIQUES AND COCKTAIL HAUNTS...

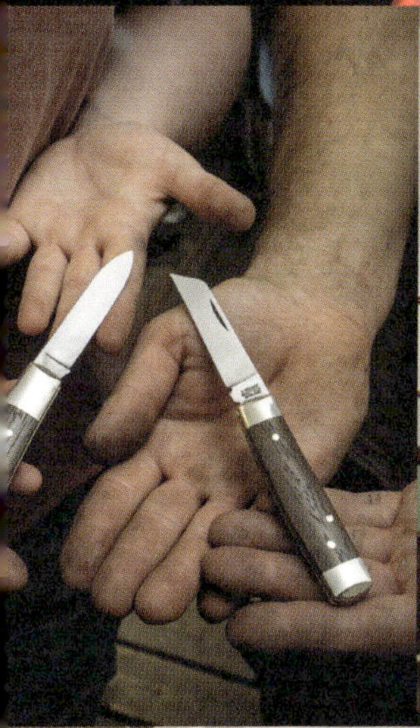

THE FAMOUS SHEFFIELD SHOP

Sheffield craftsmanship at its best

A true celebration of making heritage, The Famous Sheffield Shop showcases world-class craftsmanship from across the Steel City.

For more than four decades, The Famous Sheffield Shop has stood as a living showcase of the city's world class craftsmanship. At its location on Ecclesall Road, it's a place where Sheffield's long tradition of making continues to shine. From cutlery and tools to silverware and scissors, every item in the shop is sourced within a seven-mile radius and celebrates a lineage of skills that have shaped the city for centuries.

The shop was founded in 1983 by Don Alexander and soon grew into a destination for Sheffield-made products of every kind. Under the care of current owner Jane Summers and her experienced team, it remains an essential stop for locals and visitors alike, a compact space packed floor-to-ceiling with the very best of the city's manufacturing heritage.

Ask what's made here and the answers might surprise you. While the city's historic reputation for steel and cutlery is world famous, few realise just how much is still produced by hand. Every shelf tells part of that story: kitchen knives from Samuel Staniforth and Taylor's Eye Witness, scissors from Ernest Wright and William Whiteley and elegant cutlery from Arthur Price and William Wright. You'll also find pewter gifts from Edwin Blyde, Quirky Metals and Wentworth Pewter and carpentry tools by Joseph Marples and Robert Sorby. Even the smallest details, such as a hand-spun tankard or a polished razor, are crafted to last a lifetime.

Some designs have changed little for centuries: the Rattail cutlery pattern and the Imperial tankard remain in continuous production and have become symbols of Sheffield's blend of quality and endurance. Other pieces reflect modern innovation: contemporary designs from David Mellor and Scott Allen, jewellery from CK Crafthouse and David Scott Walker, or handmade folding pocketknives by A. Wright & Son and Michael May, now coveted by collectors across the globe.

Customers visit from every corner of the world – indeed, a map behind the till has pins tracking visits from as far afield as Hawaii and Greenland. Online orders regularly head to Europe, America and beyond, proving that the Steel City legacy continues to travel far.

The Famous Sheffield Shop
475 Ecclesall Road
S11 8PP
0114 268 5701

sheffield-made.com
@famoussheffield
Facebook: The Famous Sheffield Shop

THE FAMOUS SHEFFIELD SHOP

Closer to home, the shop serves a loyal base of Sheffielders looking for gifts for all occasions, commemorative pieces and practical tools that will last for decades. Every purchase carries a sense of continuity, a link between generations of makers and users. Engraving, polishing and restoration services are available, with more than the occasional 'Repair Shop' moment when a family heirloom is brought back to life. One recent restoration revealed a 1908 copy of The Sheffield Evening Telegraph hidden inside a cake stand base, complete with an advert for Atkinsons. A small time capsule of the past.

While production methods have modernised, the essence of Sheffield-made craftsmanship remains the same: precision, patience and pride. Techniques are still passed down through generations, with every stage – forging, polishing, plating and finishing – done by hand. The result is the high level of quality that remains in demand, whether it's Michelin-starred restaurants needing Sheffield cutlery for their dining rooms or artisans in North America looking for the most reliable tools on the market.

Beyond the products themselves, The Famous Sheffield Shop also supports local authors and photographers, including leading professional photographer Pete Hill, whose portraits of craftsmen form a visual archive of the city's skilled makers. Heritage Open Days, meet the maker events and collaborations with Sheffield designers highlight the continuing innovation within these traditional trades.

At its heart, this special spot tells the story of a city that never stopped making. Each item, whether a chef's knife, a pewter hip flask or handmade silver cufflinks, is part of an ongoing narrative of design and durability.

More than a retail space, The Famous Sheffield Shop is a bridge between past and present; a celebration of people who continue to make objects of purpose and beauty. It's proof that in Sheffield, craftsmanship is not just heritage, it's a living, evolving tradition.

The Famous Sheffield Shop
475 Ecclesall Road
S11 8PP
0114 268 5701

sheffield-made.com
@famoussheffield
Facebook: The Famous Sheffield Shop

Photography: Pete Hill

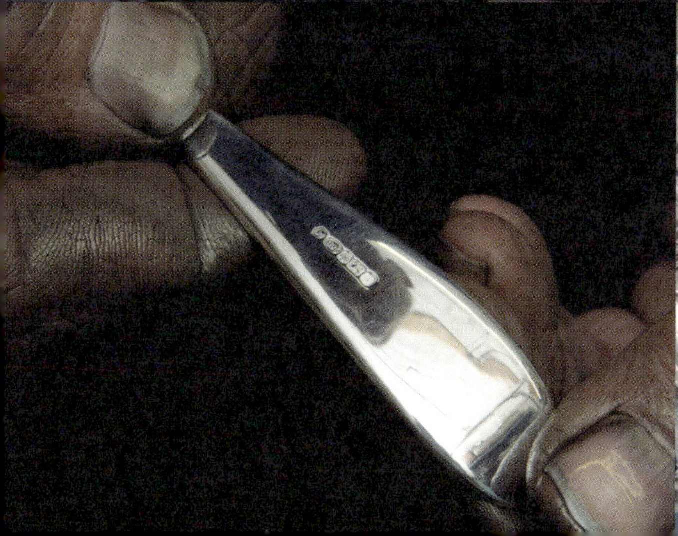

ASHOKA

Inspired by India, made in Sheffield

A true Sheffield institution, Ashoka has been serving "reyt good curreh" since 1967. Blending Indian heritage with local heart, this much-loved restaurant continues to evolve under Rahul Amin's care – proof that tradition and innovation can share the same table.

Few restaurants in Sheffield carry the same sense of history and affection as Ashoka. Opened in 1967 by Kamal Ahmed, a young Bengali entrepreneur with no prior experience in hospitality, it introduced authentic Indian cooking to a city still new to the idea of curry houses. More than half a century later, the venue remains one of Sheffield's most loved independent restaurants, continuing to evolve while staying true to its roots.

Led by owner Rahul Amin since 2004, Ashoka continues to honour the spirit that defined it from the start – "reyt good curreh", served with warmth and consistency. The restaurant's long-serving team is part of that story, many having worked there for decades. Their dedication brings a continuity that regulars cherish, giving the restaurant its familiar rhythm and unmistakable sense of belonging.

Inside, the interiors nods to the Irani cafés of Mumbai, with monochrome tiles, tiffin boxes, Sheffield-made silverware and polished wooden tables. The setting feels both nostalgic and current, reflecting the restaurant's character – steeped in heritage yet always open to new influences.

On the menu, house classics sit alongside creative specialities such as the Taxi Driver Curry, an Ashoka original. Dishes like karai, kashmiri, biryani and lamb chops are cooked over charcoal in the traditional tandoor, their aromas filling the compact dining room. The food balances comfort and authenticity, underpinned by careful spicing and quality ingredients.

Part of Ashoka's enduring appeal lies in its intimacy. With just a handful of tables, every seat feels close to the heart of the action. Whether on a busy weekend evening or a midweek service, the room hums with lively chatter and a sense of familiarity – the feeling of a restaurant that has long been part of the culinary furniture in the Steel City.

As it approaches its sixth decade, Ashoka stands as both a local institution and a continuing labour of love – inspired by India, shaped by Sheffield, and still serving plates of food that bring comfort and connection to generations of diners.

Ashoka
307 Ecclesall Road
S11 8NX
0114 268 3029

ashoka1967.com
@ashokasheffield

Photos: Ellie Grace Photography

ASHOKA
INSPIRED BY INDIA ◆ MADE IN SHEFFIELD
REYT
GOOD
CURREH

SHEFFIELD MAKERS HUNTERS BAR

Made in Sheffield

A creative hub for handcrafted design, where over 50 Sheffield makers sell unique ceramics, prints, jewellery and more in a welcoming, artist-run space.

Standing bold and bright in sunshine yellow on the corner of Ecclesall and Sharrow Vale Road is Sheffield Makers Hunters Bar – a celebration of the city's creative talent.

Stocking work from over 50 local artists, makers and designers, inside you'll find everything from hand-thrown ceramics and contemporary jewellery to prints, textiles, skincare and homewares – all made right here in Sheffield, and in many cases sold directly by the maker behind it.

The shop opened in 2018, taking over the former Jesters gift shop. The building itself has seen all sorts over the years, from a family-run bakery to an interiors store, and now it's home to a new generation of creatives. Setting it up as a separate business from its Winter Gardens sister shop gave the team freedom to grow, bringing together a wider community of artists while keeping things grounded in local values.

Its collective structure allows contributors to share responsibilities, with each member taking on shop shifts alongside their own creative work. That means visitors are always greeted by someone who knows the stock inside out – and often helped make it.

Sheffield Makers Hunters Bar is a go-to for thoughtful gifting and locally made design, but it's also a space that nurtures connection and collaboration between independent makers. Whether you're a regular looking for new work from familiar faces or just dropping in while browsing the Sharrow Vale indie strip, there's always something fresh to discover.

A proper gem for anyone keen to shop local; support Sheffield talent and pick up something beautifully made along the way.

Sheffield Makers Hunters Bar
667 Ecclesall Road
S11 8PT

@sheffieldmakers huntersbar

I'M MAKING WAFFLES
Lovely
Lovely
Lovely
Lovely
Lovely
Lovely
Lovely
Lovely
Lovely
Lovely
Lovely
Lovely
Lovely

THE PSALTER

Modern dining, Sheffield soul

The Psalter blends boutique hotel charm, modern British cooking and laidback Sheffield hospitality – a place to eat, drink and stay that feels both refined and refreshingly down-to-earth.

In leafy Sharrow, a local landmark with a storied past has been reimagined by acclaimed chef Tom Lawson. The Psalter – a boutique hotel, bar and restaurant – brings together refined dining, relaxed hospitality and that unmistakable Sheffield warmth under one elegant roof.

After stepping away from Rafters, Lawson set his sights on a long-held ambition: to open a restaurant with rooms in Sheffield's south-west. He found the perfect canvas in The Psalter – a once-loved pub and hotel that had fallen into disuse but still held plenty of charm and potential. What followed was a rapid, hands-on transformation led by Lawson himself, injecting new life and soul into the building.

Today, The Psalter is home to four distinct offerings: a 20-room hotel, a welcoming bar serving small plates, a private events space, and fine dining restaurant Tom Lawson at The Psalter, which delivers modern British cooking rooted in local, seasonal produce. Menus balance approachability with craft – think rhubarb grown in Lawson's own garden, lamb from the Wortley Estate, or flavour-packed small plates perfect for a laid-back midweek bite.

In just five months, the restaurant has already been recognised by one of the biggest names in the industry – joining the Michelin Guide in October 2025. It's a huge moment for Lawson and his team, and a testament to their commitment to quality, seasonality and warm, unpretentious service.

Set away from the bustle yet within easy reach of both the city and the Peaks, The Psalter is a place to eat well, unwind and celebrate – whether you're stopping by for a pint, a party or a seven-course tasting menu.

A new chapter for one of Nether Edge's best-known buildings – and a fresh statement of intent from one of Sheffield's most respected chefs.

The Psalter
178–180 Psalter Lane
Sharrow
S11 8US
0114 349 6956

@psaltersheffield

Psalter

THE PSALTER/TOM LAWSON

After 15 years at the helm of Rafters, one of Sheffield's most celebrated restaurants, chef-owner Tom Lawson has turned his attention to a new challenge: transforming The Psalter from a local pub into a relaxed boutique hotel and dining destination. Here, he reflects on fresh starts, Sheffield pride and building a legacy rooted in warmth, care and authenticity.

What made you decide that The Psalter was the right project for you after Rafters?

Funnily enough, the opportunity came about when my father-in-law sent me the lease listing from the local paper – half as a joke. But as soon as I looked at it, something just clicked. I'd already been searching for a new site in the area, and I knew exactly what I wanted: somewhere with rooms, off-road parking, and room to grow. The Psalter ticked every box.

What really appealed to me was that it offered a fresh start. Rafters has been a Sheffield dining institution for over three decades, and I'll always be proud of what we achieved there, but it came with a legacy. With The Psalter, I saw a blank canvas – a place with history, yes, but without a defined identity. It had never truly been a destination, and that gave me the chance to shape something from the ground up. I wanted to give it a soul and create something genuinely special for Sheffield.

Was running a hotel always part of the plan, or did the opportunity shape the dream?

Running a hotel wasn't something I had planned from the start. Restaurants are tough, especially in the current climate, and as I've grown as a businessperson, I've learned the value of diversification. The opportunity to add rooms and create a full hospitality experience felt like the natural next step.

How did you approach transforming a local pub into the destination it is now?

Building a destination with longevity takes time — this isn't a flash in the pan. From the start, our goal has been to create a Sheffield icon rooted in hospitality. Every decision, from the design to the service to the food and drink, has been about creating a cohesive experience that feels authentic, accessible, and enduring.

As a chef, what's been the biggest learning curve in running a hotel?

The biggest challenge has been seeing hospitality as a whole rather than just what's on the plate. A hotel never sleeps – there are so many moving parts. Learning to trust a team, delegate effectively, and think about the guest journey from arrival to departure has been both challenging and deeply rewarding.

How hands-on are you with the day-to-day operations outside of the kitchen?

I'm involved where it matters most, but I've learned that you can't do everything yourself. I like to understand every part of the guest experience, but I also rely on a talented team who share the same values.

THE
HOTEL

THE PSALTER/TOM LAWSON

How do you ensure a sense of continuity between the hotel, the bar, and the fine dining restaurant?

It all comes back to a single ethos: warmth, care, and authenticity. Guests should feel that whether they're in the bar, dining in the restaurant, or staying overnight, they're part of the same story.

Your menus showcase strong Sheffield roots – what does "local" mean to you in practice?

Local isn't just about ingredients; it's about community and collaboration. We work closely with producers across Sheffield and Yorkshire. Our tables are set with Sheffield cutlery from Carrs Silver, we serve our own blend gin from Locksley Distillery, and our coffee is locally roasted.

How do you balance accessibility with innovation across different dining spaces?

The key is creating experiences that excite but never intimidate. In the bar, we focus on elevated, approachable dishes and drinks; in the restaurant, we push creativity while keeping flavours familiar and enjoyable.

Are there any dishes or ingredients that you feel really capture The Psalter's spirit?

Our menus celebrate Yorkshire ingredients in ways that feel both familiar and inspired. Local venison, Sheffield honey, and Henderson's Relish are simple, honest ingredients, but used thoughtfully, they tell the story of this place.

What's your long-term vision for The Psalter?

To create a place that stands the test of time – a Sheffield destination people return to, recommend, and remember. We've just been granted our marriage licence, which makes us Sheffield's only Michelin-listed wedding venue.

Do you see this model – relaxed hotel dining with fine food – as the future of Sheffield hospitality?

Absolutely. People want experiences that feel special but not stiff or formal. Sheffield's hospitality scene is evolving toward a balance of comfort and creativity.

What do you hope guests take away from their visit, whether they're staying overnight or just stopping for a pint?

I hope they leave feeling genuinely cared for. We want people to feel they've discovered something memorable – a place that feels right, where every visit matters.

How do you see The Psalter fitting into the wider Nether Edge and Sheffield scene?

Nether Edge has a fantastic sense of community, and The Psalter is proud to be part of that. Sheffield has a strong, understated confidence, and The Psalter is built in that same spirit: approachable, authentic, and quietly ambitious.

THE PSALTER
CAR PARK AT THE REAR
the psalt
Come in we are OPEN
follow us on
@PSALTERSHEFFIELD

KUKI
NEW ZEALAND
ROASTOLOGY

SHEFFIELD FISHCAKE WITH HENDOS KETCHUP

Preparation time: 1 hour 30 minutes (including brining) | Cook time: 15 minutes | Serves: 4

Ingredients:

100g water
5g table salt
1 × 800g plaice, filleted
1 large Maris Piper potato
5g dashi crystals or dashi concentrate
2 × sheets nori seaweed
15ml dashi vinegar
25ml Henderson's Relish
2 tsp Ultratex
200g gluten-free self-raising flour
100g potato starch
200ml beer of your choice
Curry salt, for seasoning
1 lemon, zest only
12 dill fronds
10g samphire

Method:

Dissolve the salt in the water to make a brine. Submerge the plaice fillets and refrigerate for 1 hour. Rinse off the brine and pat the fish dry with kitchen paper. Cut into eight pieces, each about 40 × 20mm.

Using a mandoline, slice the potato into 5mm-thick slices and cut four rectangles measuring 40 × 20mm. Place in a saucepan with the dashi crystals and cover with water. Bring to the boil and cook until tender but not falling apart. Drain on kitchen paper and refrigerate until needed.

Sandwich one piece of potato between two pieces of fish, then roll each in a sheet of nori to form neat parcels.

Whisk together the dashi vinegar, Henderson's Relish and Ultratex until smooth. Transfer to a piping bag and set aside.

In a large bowl, whisk together the gluten-free self-raising flour, potato starch and beer until smooth.

Heat the deep-fat fryer to 180°C. Carefully coat each fishcake in the batter and lower into the hot oil. Fry for 5–6 minutes, or until golden and crisp. Drain on kitchen paper.

Season the fishcakes with curry salt and lemon zest. Arrange on serving plates, then pipe small dots of the Henderson's Relish ketchup on top of each. Garnish with dill fronds and samphire.

Serve immediately.

The Psalter
178–180 Psalter Lane
Sharrow
S11 8US
0114 349 6956

@psaltersheffield

TURNIP & THYME

British comfort food with family at its heart

A much-loved neighbourhood bistro run by a sibling team, serving thoughtful, seasonal dishes prepared with warmth – a place where quality ingredients and hospitality take centre stage.

Located near Hunter's Bar on Ecclesall Road, Turnip & Thyme has become one of Sheffield's most cherished neighbourhood bistros. Run by brother-and-sister team Louise and Robert, it blends the warmth of a family kitchen with the polish of a well-run restaurant, earning praise from locals and visitors alike.

Since opening six years ago, the pair have built a loyal following for their modern take on British comfort food – the sort of cooking that feels both nostalgic and fresh. The menu changes with the seasons, but its foundations remain the same: honest, generous dishes made properly and served without fuss. Robert leads the kitchen, turning out favourites such as slow-cooked pork belly, beef Wellington and perfectly crisp Sunday roasts, while Louise runs front of house with calm assurance and a personal touch that keeps regulars coming back.

The restaurant's approach sits between bistro dining and home-style comfort. Everything is made from scratch, with ingredients sourced from trusted local suppliers, from Derbyshire meats to Sheffield gins and small-batch ice cream makers. The restaurant's themed evenings have become highlights of the local dining calendar: Seafood Nights every Tuesday and Wednesday focus on sustainably caught fish and shellfish, while the final Thursday of each month brings Steak Night, featuring Tomahawk or Chateaubriand cuts made for sharing.

By the weekend, the focus turns to one of the best Sunday roasts in the city, complete with towering Yorkshire puddings, rich gravy and a sense of occasion that still feels relaxed and familiar. Many diners travel across Sheffield just for the roasts, often booking weeks in advance to guarantee a table.

The restaurant's interior mirrors its menu – warm, comfortable and welcoming, with soft lighting and rustic wooden tables that invite guests to slow down and enjoy the experience. Beyond the dining room, the team also cater for weddings, family gatherings and private dinners, bringing the same care and consistency to each event.

Grounded, generous and full of heart, Turnip & Thyme continues to thrive as a local favourite – a celebration of good food, genuine hospitality and the simple pleasure of sharing a meal.

Turnip & Thyme
740 Ecclesall Road
S11 8TB
0114 266 1510

www.
turnipandthyme.co.uk
@turnipandthyme

TURNIP & THYME

GIFT VOUCHERS

SPICED SALMON WITH COUSCOUS & POMEGRANATE SALSA

This vibrant dish from Turnip & Thyme brings together beautifully spiced salmon, fluffy giant couscous, and a fresh, zesty pomegranate salsa. It's a perfect balance of warmth, colour, and texture – ideal for an easy midweek meal that still feels special.

Preparation time: 15 minutes | Cooking time: 15 minutes | Serves: 2

Ingredients

For the salsa

1 red onion, diced
100g pomegranate seeds
1 lime, zested and juiced
A handful of fresh mint, chopped
1 tbsp olive oil
Salt and pepper, to season

For the spice mix

½ tsp ground cinnamon
½ tsp ground cumin
½ tsp ground coriander
½ tsp paprika

For the couscous

150g giant couscous
1 tbsp olive oil
½ lemon, juiced
A handful each of chopped fresh parsley, fresh mint & fresh chives

For the salmon

2 salmon fillets
Salt and pepper, to season
20g butter
1 tbsp spice mix (from above)
½ lime, for squeezing

Method

Preheat the oven to 180°c.

For the salsa

To make the salsa, combine the diced red onion, pomegranate seeds, lime zest and juice, chopped mint, and olive oil in a bowl. Season well and set aside to allow the flavours to develop.

For the spice mix and cous cous

For the spice mix, stir together the ground cinnamon, cumin, coriander, and paprika in a small bowl.

Bring a pan of salted water to the boil and blanch the giant couscous for 9 minutes. Drain well, then immediately toss with the olive oil, lemon juice, and chopped herbs. Keep warm while you prepare the salmon.

For the salmon

Season the salmon fillets with salt, pepper, and a sprinkle of the spice mix. Heat a nonstick frying pan over a low-medium heat with some olive oil. Place the salmon skin side down and cook for 4 to 5 minutes, until the skin is crisp. Flip the fillets and transfer the pan to the oven for 6 minutes, or until the fish feels firm to the touch.

Return the pan to the hob, add the butter and 1 tablespoon of the spice mix, and baste the salmon as it melts. Finish with a squeeze of lime.

To serve

Serve the salmon on a bed of warm couscous and spoon the pomegranate salsa generously over the top.

Turnip & Thyme
740 Ecclesall Road
S11 8TB
0114 266 1510

www.turnipandthyme.co.uk
@turnipandthyme

CAFFÈ TUCCI

Napoli ever after

An Italian café duo bringing the warmth, flavour and everyday rituals of Naples to Sheffield through fresh food, great coffee and southern (Italian!) charm.

When brothers Stefano and Salvatore Capasso arrived from Naples, they brought more than just the flavours of their hometown – they brought its spirit.

Warm, expressive and driven by a shared love of food and people, their two award-winning Caffè Tucci venues have become modern Sheffield institutions, known for serving up a slice of everyday Italian life with genuine southern charm.

Their first café opened on Surrey Street in early 2022, and quickly became a favourite for its expertly poured Italian coffee, build-your-own panini counter and the unmistakable buzz of Neapolitan hospitality. Two years later, a second site on Ecclesall Road allowed the brothers to expand their culinary ambitions. With a larger kitchen, they've introduced a broader menu of freshly made Italian dishes – rich lasagne, slow-cooked meatballs and the kind of hearty street foods found on the lively backstreets of Naples.

Step inside either Caffè Tucci and you'll find a space that feels both homely and distinctly Neapolitan. Walls are adorned with Italian football scarves, family photos and tributes to their city's most iconic figure, Diego Maradona. The décor captures the essence of a true neighbourhood café – casual and full of character – with the scent of espresso and fresh focaccia in the air and the sound of friendly chatter carrying through from the counter.

Cooking runs deep in the Capasso family. Their father was a chef for more than 40 years, and Stefano still recalls making his first parmigiana under his dad's watchful eye at the age of eight. That sense of craft and connection defines everything they do. Each Caffè Tucci is as much about community as cuisine – a place to pause, talk and feel at home.

The Ecclesall Road site now serves a small but carefully curated pasta lunch menu – available Monday to Friday – featuring two or three varieties of homemade pasta made fresh each day. The brothers' mission is simple: good food, fair prices and a welcome that feels as warm as the southern Italian sun.

Caffè Tucci
655 Ecclesall Road
S11 8PT
&
49 Surrey Street
S1 2LG
@caffe_tucci_sheffield

Caffè Tucci

I Caffè Tucci

THE WONKY LABRADOR

A welcoming micropub with character and heart

A small pub with big personality. Craft beers, cocktails and a strong sense of community make this colourful Fulwood favourite a warm, inclusive spot for good company.

Tucked away on leafy Oakbrook Road in Fulwood, The Wonky Labrador has fast become one of Sheffield's most distinctive micropubs. Small in size but big on personality, it offers a relaxed space where craft beer enthusiasts, wine lovers and weekend cocktail drinkers all feel at home.

Run by owner Mac McGrath – whose two decades in hospitality and love of European and New Zealand pub culture inspired him to create something different for the Steel City – the bar has been transformed since he took over in March 2023. It's now a warm, characterful hangout that feels both familiar and new. Inside, you'll find snug seating and friendly chatter, while the cosy beer garden offers a solid al fresco option. With hand-painted murals by local artist The Moody Violet and a carefully chosen drinks list, the space radiates comfort, colour and feelgood vibes.

Eight rotating keg lines showcase an ever-changing selection of local and international beers, including gluten-free options that reflect Mac's own coeliac journey. Alongside them sits a thoughtful range of organic wines, small-batch spirits and well-executed classic cocktails, all offered at fair prices.

With a commitment to serving the community, The Wonky Labrador has quickly established itself as something of a mini events hub. Regular get-togethers include cinema nights, games evenings – playing everything from retro board games to new consoles – and mental health safe-space sessions that make inclusivity a part of the pub's DNA. The venue is proudly LGBTQ+ friendly and welcomes everyone, from families and dog walkers to first-time visitors.

The name carries its own charm, inspired by a beloved family Labrador from Mac's childhood – and to date, it remains the only public house in the world bearing that distinctive name. Naturally the pub mascot is their very own in-house Labrador puppy, Scout, who even shares a bloodline with the original Wonky Lab!

With its easygoing atmosphere, curated drinks selection and strong sense of duty to its patrons, The Wonky Labrador has earned its reputation as one of Fulwood's friendliest corners – proof that the best pubs are built on heart as much as hops.

The Wonky Labrador
212 Oakbrook Road
S11 7ED

thewonkylabrador.co.uk
@thewonkylabrador

THE WONKY LABRADOR
MICROBAR
www.feathersandlashes.com

Evans Lee

ABBEYDALE ROAD & CHESTERFIELD ROAD

Our final stop on the tour takes us southwest down Abbeydale Road and Chesterfield Road – two long, lively stretches packed with history, character and some of the best food and drink Sheffield has to offer.

Abbeydale Road has seen a real resurgence in recent years. Once an old coaching route into the city, it's now one of Sheffield's go-to spots for a night out. There's a proper run of boozers along here – from The Broadfield with its top-notch pies and pints, to Two Thirds, Dead Donkey, The Bear and plenty more in between. By day, the stretch is full of life – indie cafés, vintage shops, galleries and eateries that reflect the area's diverse community.

And then there's the Abbeydale Picture House. A grand old landmark built in 1920 and once known as the "Picture Palace" of Sheffield. It's now being lovingly restored by the team at True North, who are breathing new life into the venue while keeping its original charm intact. When it's fully reopened, it'll be a proper cultural gem once again – cinema, events, gigs and more under that iconic vaulted ceiling.

Chesterfield Road continues that vibe. Originally laid as a turnpike in 1757 to replace the old Derby route, it now stretches all the way out of town, dotted with indie cafés, proper pubs and long-standing locals. Areas like Heeley and Meersbrook grew up around this road – once farmland, now tightly packed terraces, with Meersbrook Park and Graves Park offering leafy breathing space on either side. The railway arrived in 1870 and helped the area boom, transforming the Sheaf Valley into one of Sheffield's busiest arteries.

It's a stretch that still feels lived in and looked after – so let's take a stroll down each and meet some of the people making Abbeydale and Chesterfield Roads what they are today...

ONCE AN OLD COACHING ROUTE INTO THE CITY, IT'S NOW ONE OF SHEFFIELD'S GO-TO SPOTS FOR A NIGHT OUT...

THE GIN BAR
SPARKLERS

TWO THIRDS
TWO THIRDS BEER CO.

THE BEAR

THE BOSTON ARMS

Small in size, big in character

A bustling spot shaking up Woodseats' drinking scene, The Boston Arms blends big flavour with small-pub charm – where craft beer meets cocktail creativity, and there's something for everyone on the menu.

Nestled in a cosy corner of Chesterfield Road in Woodseats, The Boston Arms has quickly become a local favourite. Since opening its doors in May 2022, this dog-friendly micropub has built a loyal following and was named Best Micropub at the 2025 Exposed Magazine Awards – a testament to the atmosphere, quality and care poured into every pint and cocktail.

Keen to champion northern produce, The Boston's beer offering spans eight keg lines and three cask lines, featuring a mix of local breweries and iconic names. Permanent lines include Abbeydale's Moonshine pale ale on cask, Triple Point's Helles lager and Thornbridge's Green Mountain IPA on keg. The team are committed to keeping the range diverse and accessible, with two core gluten-free options always available.

Setting itself apart from its counterparts, however, is a superb selection of cocktails – carefully curated and seasonally rotating. A far cry from the pre-mixed cartons you might expect from pubs, the menu features over 20 cocktails made with in-house syrups and infused spirits. While the bar originally focused mainly on craft beer, its growing popularity has seen cocktails step confidently into the spotlight, now sharing equal billing.

Although the The Boston is no longer the only venue in Woodseats offering craft cocktails, it was the first to introduce this kind of offering to the area. The latest menu keeps fan favourites such as the Cherry Bakewell Sour and Spicy Margarita, alongside new creations designed to surprise regulars and newcomers alike.

A new avenue the team are exploring is beer cocktails – merging their two main offerings and blurring the lines to create playful, distinctive drinks. One example is the Mocha Stoutini, which combines stout and chocolate to deliver a smooth, decadent twist on the classic espresso martini.

As Woodseats continues to evolve, The Boston Arms remains one of its most vibrant social spots – independent, welcoming and always open to trying something new. With its range of craft beer, locally roasted coffee, homemade pizzas and inventive cocktail menu, it's easy to see why the people of Sheffield voted this their favourite.

The Boston Arms
676 Chesterfield Road
S8 0SD

@bostonarms.sheffield

WING
2-4-1
STONE
BREWING
Lambicus

WALTER
LAYLA♡
YODA
ANNIE
Norman
KAYLEE
TOBY♡
MOOSE
STANLEY
SOX
JAFFA
PEGGY♡
WILLOW

HOT &
FRESH
PIZZA

THE BOSTON
ARMS

GREEN MOUNTAIN HAZY IPA
VERDITA JUICY SOUR
KING OF TERRORS NEIPA
SALVATION PARKIN STOUT GF
DRAUGHT CASK
MOONSHINE PALE GF
PILGRIM PUMPKIN SPICED ALE GF
BLACK BAND PORTER

MOCHA STOUTINI

Rich, velvety and indulgent, this Mocha Stoutini brings together espresso, chocolate stout, and smooth spirits for a bold twist on the classic espresso martini. With its creamy froth and deep mocha notes, this cocktail is a guaranteed showstopper.

Preparation time: 5 minutes | Makes 1 cocktail

Ingredients

25ml vodka (or aged rum)

12.5ml chocolate stout syrup (see below)

12.5ml crème de cacao

50ml stout

35ml espresso

2 dashes of Fee Brother's chocolate bitters

¼ pipette of Ms. Better's Bitters (optional)

Ice cubes

Equipment

Boston cocktail shaker

Hawthorne strainer

Fine mesh strainer

25ml/50ml jigger

Coupe glass

Method

Add all the ingredients to a cocktail shaker, followed by plenty of ice.

Shake hard for about 10 seconds, then double strain into a chilled coupe glass.

Garnish with coffee beans or a drizzle of chocolate syrup.

Chocolate Stout Syrup

Add 500ml chocolate stout to a saucepan and cook over a medium heat until reduced by half.

Weigh the remaining liquid and add twice the amount of demerara sugar.

Return to the heat, stirring until all the sugar has dissolved.

Leave to cool, then remove any layer that forms on the surface.

Store at room temperature in an airtight container for up to 2 weeks.

Bartender's Notes

Double straining – using both the Hawthorne and fine mesh strainers – ensures no small shards of ice make their way into the cocktail.

Ms. Better's Bitters are optional; they don't alter the flavour but help create a long-lasting frothy head.

Cold brew concentrate can be used in place of freshly brewed espresso if preferred.

Always add ice to the shaker last to control dilution and avoid shocking the espresso, which can cause bitterness.

The Boston Arms
676 Chesterfield Road
S8 0SD

@bostonarms.sheffield

THE BARE ALTERNATIVE

Individual actions can add up to bigger change

This pioneering refill shop champions sustainability, affordability and community – making it easier for Sheffielders to shop responsibly and reduce waste, one refill at a time.

Nestled among the independent shops of Abbeydale Road, The Bare Alternative has quietly become one of the region's leading low-impact retailers. Founded in 2018 by Mathew Reynolds, the shop began with a simple idea: to make sustainable shopping affordable and practical for everyone.

What started as a small refill store moved to new premises in 2020, gradually evolving into South Yorkshire's largest low-waste and refill shopping destination with a wide range of products all under one roof. Customers bring their own containers to refill everything from dried foods, grains and spices to household cleaners, soaps and personal care items. The approach not only reduces packaging waste but also encourages a slower, more mindful way to shop.

Since its early days, The Bare Alternative has helped customers save thousands of kilograms of single-use plastic from entering circulation. Mathew recently calculated that if all the goods sold in the shop last year had been bought in typical supermarket packaging, they would have generated almost three and a half tonnes of plastic waste. That figure represents a tangible difference – a clear sign that small, consistent actions really do add up.

The shop's ethos centres on three key values of sustainability, affordability and accessibility. Products are carefully sourced from ethical suppliers with strong environmental credentials, many of them based in the UK. From bamboo toothbrushes to plastic-free deodorants and eco detergents delivered in a closed-loop system, every detail supports a circular approach.

Customer connection is a big part of what keeps the shop thriving. Regulars come not just to refill, but to chat with the team, swap tips and discover new products. It's as much a community hub as a shop – a space where people can relax and explore sustainability at their own pace. Without places like The Bare Alternative, the local community would be left with little choice but to turn to supermarkets, where buying goods inevitably means going home with the packaging too.

Now in its seventh year, the business continues to grow, guided by the same principles that inspired it from the start: helping people live more sustainably without making it complicated or costly.

The Bare Alternative
332 Abbeydale Road
S7 1FN
07422 405166

barealternative.co.uk
@barealternative

SUSTAINABLE SWAPS

THE BARE ALTERNATIVE

soap bar
Eco Sponge Scourer
compostable sponge cloths

Lemon Balm

THE BEAR

Craft beer, character and community on tap

The Bear is a small but lively craft beer bar a welcoming hangout where great beer, good conversation and Sheffield's independent soul flow side by side.

Found at the start of Abbeydale Road's strip of independents, The Bear has become one of Sheffield's most distinctive craft beer destinations. When Matt Beety opened it in 2021, the original idea was a modest bottle shop – but it quickly evolved into something far more social.

What started as a space to browse, chat and pick up takeaway cans soon turned into a small but buzzing bar, where people wanted to linger, talk and explore what was pouring. Over time, it's grown into a relaxed hangout spot with the feel of a living room – a place where strangers share tables, friendships form and regulars jokingly refer to themselves as the "Bear Fam".

Inside, the space is snug and welcoming, with seating for around 30 and room for more on their terrace. Behind the bar, six keg lines and one cask line keep things constantly changing. New beers arrive almost daily, ranging from local favourites to ambitious imports from across Europe and the US. Around 300 bottles and cans line the fridges and shelves, ensuring there's always something new to discover.

Matt's focus has always been on approachability – breaking down the barriers that can sometimes surround craft beer culture. Staff are encouraged to talk about flavour and style without jargon, helping people find what they love rather than what they think they should order. It's this friendly, inclusive approach that has helped The Bear stand out on a road known for its independents.

The bar also hosts lively events that bring people together – from "Meet the Brewer" evenings with top UK and European breweries to creative collaborations like wine and crisp pairings. These intimate nights often sell out within hours and have become a signature part of what makes the venue special.

Despite its size, The Bear has built something much bigger than itself – a close-knit, welcoming venue that reflects the best of Sheffield's independent spirit. It's a place to pop in for a browse, stay for a chat and feel part of something genuine.

The Bear
89 Abbeydale Road
S7 1FE
07765 223061

@thebearsheffield
thebearbeer.com

THE BEAR

THE BEAR

TALOS
MEGAERA
NYX
BEAK
Obeisance

THE BEAR
THE BEAR
THE BEAR

ALL CARROT NO STICK

Proudly vegan, rooted in community

All Carrot No Stick is a proudly vegan, community-minded shop championing local makers and sustainable living. Stocking everything from plant-based essentials to refill products, it's a warm, ethical hub where good food, friendly faces and conscious choices come together.

A fixture on Chesterfield Road for decades, the site now home to All Carrot No Stick has long been part of Sheffield's independent shopping story. The space was first transformed into a 100% vegan shop back in 2016, and later became All Carrot No Stick during the pandemic – with a simple aim: to create a welcoming, ethical space for conscious consumers and local makers alike.

Inside, shelves are lined with everything from plant-based cheeses, chocolate and tofu to locally made sauces, breads and soaps. The team work closely with Sheffield producers, stocking favourites like Bullion Chocolate, Birdhouse Tea, Henderson's Relish, Four Eyes Patisserie and Forge Coffee Roasters. There's a strong gluten-free range too, and a growing selection of refillable household products, making it a one-stop shop for anyone who values sustainable living and quality local produce.

What sets All Carrot No Stick apart is its sense of community. Regulars pop in not just to shop but to chat, swap recommendations and see what new independent brands have arrived. The friendly, down-to-earth atmosphere gives the shop the feel of an old-fashioned grocer with a modern, planet-conscious twist – a space where conversations with friends matter as much as the products themselves.

The shop's loyalty scheme, the Carrot Club, adds a bit of fun to the mix, rewarding customers with points that can be redeemed or donated to local causes such as Food Works and Charlie's Place Animal Sanctuary, both of which the shop proudly supports. Collaborations with small producers and creatives in the area have helped turn it into a genuine community hub – somewhere local businesses champion one another and customers feel part of something bigger.

After nearly five decades of independent, eco-conscious retail on the same site, All Carrot No Stick continues to fly the flag for local, ethical shopping – a hub for the community in S8, reflecting the creativity and collaboration that define the area's independent spirit. Warm, welcoming and full of character, it's proof that small shops can make a big difference – one refill, friendly chat and bar of vegan chocolate at a time.

All Carrot No Stick
31 Chesterfield Road
S8 0RL
07525 055656

allcarrotsheffield@gmail.com
allcarrotnostick.co.uk
FB: AllCarrotNoStick
Insta: @allcarrotnostick

BULLION
TRADE MARK
CHOCOLATE MAKERS
2016
Seville Orange

OH, GRATE!
PARVEGGIO
Sheese
Sheese
VINTAGE
Sheese
SHEESE

FORGE
COFFEE ROASTERS
MMXV

All Carrot No Stick

BENCH

Warming the communal bench

In Nether Edge, Bench brings people together around food, drink and conversation. What began as a pop-up is now a relaxed neighbourhood spot known for its seasonal small plates, natural wines and easy warmth.

What started as a pop-up supper club back in 2018 has since settled into one of Sheffield's most quietly confident food spots. Tucked away in leafy Nether Edge, Bench is a neighbourhood hangout where everything from the menu to the mood feels considered but never fussy.

Run by Jack Wakelin and exec chef Tom 'Ronnie' Aronica, Bench made the leap from temporary tables to a permanent home in 2020, turning a former barbershop into a stylishly stripped-back bistro and bar. The space is centred around communal bench seating – a nod to its name and ethos – encouraging a kind of casual conviviality that's increasingly rare.

On the plate, it's all about seasonal, thoughtful cooking with a knack for balancing comfort and creativity. Expect bold flavours, inventive small plates and an evolving menu that leans into fire cooking, neglected cuts, and influences from Ronnie's Italian heritage. There's a playfulness to the food here, but it's backed by serious skill and a clear love of good ingredients.

Drinks-wise, the natural wine list is a standout, joined by sharp cocktails and local beers – the sort of bar setup you'll happily settle into whether or not you came to eat. In warmer months, the outdoor terrace is a favourite with locals, pint in hand and snacks within easy reach.

Bench isn't trying to be a destination – and that's exactly why it's become one. It feels rooted, relaxed and refreshingly Sheffield, a place you'll find yourself returning to for after-work drinks, weekend meals or long-overdue catch-ups. Smart but unpretentious, familiar but surprising – the kind of spot every neighbourhood wishes it had.

Bench
7b Nether Edge Road
S7 1RU
0114 3221020

@benchsheffield
benchsheffield.co.uk

Photography: India Hobson

COCKTAILS — WINE — BISTRO — SHOP

La Cave

THE LITTLE BOOK OF
SHEFFIELD 2025

AROUND TOWN

Of course, there's more to Sheffield than the neighbourhoods we've listed – there's plenty happening beyond the well-travelled routes, and you'll find brilliant independents popping up in every corner of the city.

From tucked-away producers to destination restaurants that sit just off the radar, this final chapter celebrates the indies doing great things in places you might not pass through every day – but should absolutely make time for.

Up north, Oughtibridge and Ecclesfield are home to everything from city-defining chefs to quirky gift shops, all working with the same passion and creativity you'll find at the heart of the city. Some are based in quiet industrial units, others in converted mills and edge-of-town workshops – and while they're tucked away, they hold their own against anything in the city's busiest postcodes.

Head south and you'll soon find yourself where the city gives way to rolling fields and family-run farms. It's here you'll find producers like Moss Valley Meats – raising some of the region's best pork on land that's been worked for generations. It's peaceful, hard-grafting and deeply rooted in place – everything good food should be.

So before we wrap things up, here's one last detour – a celebration of the places that sit slightly out of view but always deliver. You might need a car, a walk or a bit of planning to get there – but trust us, it's worth it.

Let's meet the makers, movers and memorable spots doing it their own way – all around town.

FROM TUCKED-AWAY PRODUCERS TO DESTINATION RESTAURANTS, THIS CHAPTER CELEBRATES THE INDIES DOING GREAT THINGS IN PLACES YOU MIGHT NOT PASS THROUGH EVERY DAY

BRADFIELD
BREWERY

JÖRO

Fine dining 2.0

Now settled in a stunning riverside paper mill in Oughtibridge, Jöro continues to push Sheffield's dining scene forward. Led by Luke French and Stacey Sherwood-French, it's a place where fire, craft and creativity meet – fine dining reimagined with Northern soul and quiet confidence.

Having already redefined Sheffield's modern dining scene from a shipping container in Kelham Island, Jöro has levelled up. Now set within a beautifully restored 19th-century paper mill in Oughtibridge, the restaurant's new home matches its ambition: bold, refined and unmistakably rooted in place.

Chef Luke French and managing director Stacey Sherwood-French have created something that feels both elevated and grounded. The new site – all exposed brick, steel, wood and light – sits beside the River Don, blending industrial heritage with serene natural beauty. Inside, an open kitchen and elegant dining space set the tone for what's to come: fire-cooked dishes, Nordic and Japanese influences, and the very best of British produce treated with serious care.

Jöro isn't a place for decision fatigue – it's tasting menu only, available in three lengths, allowing the kitchen to showcase creativity while guests sit back and enjoy the ride. It's seasonal, often surprising and always beautifully executed, with a focus on flavour and finesse.

Despite the accolades (and they've plenty), Jöro doesn't trade in pretension. There's no white tablecloths, no hushed tones – just confident cooking and Northern hospitality served up with polish. Fancy without being fussy.

Upstairs, four boutique bedrooms make it easy to turn a special meal into a full evening escape – no taxi required. And with a reputation that extends far beyond Sheffield, this is a destination restaurant in the best possible sense: one that still feels like it belongs here.

At its heart, Jöro is all about balance – between past and present, city and nature, fire and finesse. Whether you're marking a milestone or just want to see what the Sheffield food scene looks like at full tilt, this is the table worth booking.

Jöro
Oughtibridge Mill
Main Road
Wharncliffe Side
S35 0LB

@restaurant_joro
jororestaurant.co.uk

Photography:
Tim Green

GREETALY

Blending the best of the Med

Blending Greek warmth with Italian flair, Greetaly brings a taste of the Mediterranean to Oughtibridge. Lively, welcoming and rooted in family tradition, it's a place where good food and company always come first.

In the heart of Oughtibridge, cosy two-floored café/restaurant Greetaly regularly fills the air with the scent of fresh focaccia, grilled meats and rich Italian coffee. This vibrant spot on Langsett Road South draws diners from across the city and beyond with a menu that unites Greek and Italian family cooking, celebrating Mediterranean flavour, warmth and the spirit of true independent dining.

The idea came from restaurateur Michael Hayes, and Italian chef Danilo Mirko Maugeri, both well known in Sheffield's food scene. Michael previously launched Sapore, Urban Pizza Co. and The Greek, ventures that helped inspire this next step. Together with the families' Italian and Greek roots, they've created a restaurant where both cuisines meet naturally, meaning that punters are never short on choice.

Everything at Greetaly is made from scratch each day. The menu – shaped with help from both sides of the family – is packed with recipes passed down through generations. Parents, aunts and uncles have flown in from Italy and Greece to train the kitchen in sauces, lasagnes and traditional Greek dishes such as feta pies, zucchini fritters and moussaka. In total, around 25 dishes from each side of the Med are on offer, inviting diners to mix and match as they please.

Drinks follow the same theme, showcasing Italian wines, Greek beers and house cocktails made with a Mediterranean twist. Desserts such as baklava and pistachio tiramisu round things off perfectly.

Downstairs, a laid-back café open daily from 9am serves espresso, pastries and rustic Italian sandwiches, along with Bullion Chocolate brownies baked fresh each morning – perfect paired with their famous hot chocolates. An Italian afternoon tea has also just been launched, with advance booking recommended given the spot's growing popularity.

Housed in a quaint, rustic building, the venue brings warmth and charm to Oughtibridge's growing foodie scene. Welcoming and full of character, it remains rooted in family, fuelled by flavour and alive with Mediterranean spirit – a true celebration of connection, community and seriously good cooking.

Greetaly
7-9 Langsett Road S
Oughtibridge
S35 0GY
0114 3221020

@thegreetaly

GREETALY
GREETALY

POLKA DOTT

A spot of craft, cake and community in Ecclesfield

This warm, characterful shop offers handmade gifts, homewares and locally baked treats, alongside regular workshops and book clubs that make it a true social hub for the neighbourhood.

More than just a lifestyle store, Polka Dott has become the welcoming heart of Ecclesfield – a cosy, creative haven where locals pop in for a chinwag, a slice of cake or to treat themselves or their loved ones to unique, handmade gifts. From a prominent spot on the high street, it's become a go-to for crafts, conversation and good company – the sort of place where familiar faces greet you at the door, and new ones never stay strangers for long.

What began with upcycled furniture sold from a family dining room has grown into a warm, characterful space brimming with handmade homewares, personalised prints, locally sourced gifts and artisan cards. The shop is run by Emma Fowler and her mum, Debra Travis, who opened the doors together in 2019 – and it's thanks to their welcoming, friendly approach, along with sister Tori's help, that they've built such a loyal following, one that stuck with them through lockdown and beyond.

Step inside and you'll find Emma there most days (with her ever-present dog, Rosie, by her side), chatting with regulars and prepping for the next craft workshop or book club. Her mum's cakes – once served from a single table in the middle of the shop – are now a local staple, with customers coming back for coffee, a catch-up and a slice of her famous flapjack. The shop feels more like a modern-day equivalent of the caffs and pubs of years gone by – a social hub, and a place for stories, laughter and support.

Workshops run throughout the year and play a big part in what makes Polka Dott special. From creative sessions to bookish get-togethers, they offer space to meet like-minded souls and try something new. Whether you're after a thoughtful gift, a hot drink or just a bit of company, Polka Dott is the kind of place that meets you where you are – and always makes you feel at home.

Polka Dott
66 High Street
Ecclesfield
S35 9XD

@polkadott_shop

Piccalilli
EMPORIUM
Chilli Jam
EMPORIUM
Bay't Warmin' Red

MOSS VALLEY FINE MEATS

Pork with provenance

Run by the Thompson family, this picturesque farm is built on high welfare, low waste and genuine craftsmanship.

Perched on the border between Sheffield and North East Derbyshire, Moss Valley Fine Meats is a fifth-generation family farm with a reputation for doing things properly – high welfare, low impact and full of flavour. At a time when we're all more conscious of where our food comes from, it strikes the perfect balance between respecting tradition and embracing innovation – producing exceptional pork that's as sustainable as it is delicious.

Run by Stephen and Karen Thompson, with their son Oliver now stepping into the fold, the farm continues a legacy over 100 years in the making. It supplies many of Sheffield's best-loved restaurants, cafés and shops with top-quality pork products, all raised and butchered just a few miles from the city.

Animal welfare sits at the heart of the operation. The pigs are raised to the highest standards, and the farm boasts one of the lowest rates of antibiotic use in the country. It's not just about great-tasting meat – it's about doing right by the animals and the environment too.

Sustainability is built into the system. The biomass boiler heats three houses, while the wider farm runs on solar, wind and closed-loop farming. That includes using pig muck to fertilise the fields that grow the crops which feed the pigs – reducing chemical use and creating a healthier, more sustainable cycle from soil to sausage.

The product range covers everything from joints, burgers and bacon to bangers made with their own signature blends. And with recent investment in the butchery, cooked meats like ham and black pudding are now part of the offering – perfect for chefs and home cooks alike.

Award-winning and proudly independent, Moss Valley Fine Meats champions short supply chains, top-tier traceability and close ties with local chefs and food producers. It's a shining example of how farming can be both forward-thinking and deeply rooted – with better meat as the result.

Moss Valley Fine Meats
Povey Farm
Lightwood Lane
S8 8BG
0114 239 9922

@mossvalleyfinemeats

EST.2022
CHOP SHOP
BAR & GRILL

BABY BACK RIBS

Located in the heart of Kelham Island, Chop Shop Bar & Grill serves up quality British cooking with a focus on locally sourced meat cooked over an Argentinian asado grill. This recipe uses a rack of Moss Valley's baby back pork ribs.

Cooking time: 2 hours 15 minutes | Serves: 4

There's something irresistible about tender, fall-off-the-bone ribs coated in a sticky, smoky glaze. These slow-cooked ribs combine spice, sweetness, and a kick of Hendos for the ultimate comfort dish.

Ingredients

For the Hendos glaze:
2 tbsp maple syrup
2 tbsp Henderson's Relish
1 tbsp soy sauce

For the pork rub:
1 tbsp Chinese five spice
2 tbsp soft brown sugar
1 tbsp garlic powder
1 tsp each salt & chilli powder
½ tsp ground black pepper
1 tsp mustard powder
1 tsp ground cumin

For the ribs:
1 rack Moss Valley baby back pork ribs
330ml Pepsi
200ml apple juice
200ml chicken stock
100ml barbecue sauce

To serve:
Crispy onions
Chopped chives

Method

Preheat the oven to 190°c.

Make the Hendos glaze:

In a small saucepan, combine the maple syrup, Hendos, and soy sauce. Heat gently for 2 to 3 minutes until slightly thickened, then set aside.

Prepare the ribs:

Mix all the pork rub ingredients in a small bowl. Rub the mixture generously over the ribs, ensuring they're well coated.

Heat a solid-top or large frying pan over a medium-high heat and sear the ribs on both sides until nicely coloured.

Cook the ribs:

Place the Pepsi, apple juice, chicken stock, barbecue sauce, and 2 tablespoons of the prepared Hendos glaze into a deep ovenproof dish. Add the seared ribs and any remaining rub, ensuring the ribs are mostly submerged in the liquid.

Cover tightly with foil and cook in the preheated oven for 2 hours, until the ribs are tender and starting to pull away from the bone.

Remove the foil and baste the ribs with some of the cooking glaze. Return to the oven uncovered for 10 to 15 minutes to allow the glaze to thicken and become sticky.

Serve the rack of ribs brushed with the remaining Hendos glaze and topped with crispy onions and chopped chives.

Moss Valley Fine Meats
Povey Farm
Lightwood Lane
S8 8BG
0114 239 9922
@mossvalleyfinemeats

S'Mores Brownie (v) / £7
Marshmallow chocolate brownie with
clotted cream ice cream.
STEAK SAUC
EST.2022
HABANERO
CHILLI SAUCE

SHEFFIELD FOOD TOURS

The best way to taste the city

Sheffield Food Tours, founded by Sophie Barber, offer a delicious way to explore the city's independent food scene. From Kelham Island to the city centre, each guided walk features local eateries, brewers and hidden gems, blending great food with local history.

Whether you're a long-time local or new to the Steel City, Sheffield Food Tours offer a delicious deep dive into the city's thriving independent food scene. Founded by passionate foodie Sophie Barber, these guided strolls combine great eats with local insight and a sprinkling of Sheffield history, making them the ideal way to discover the city one bite at a time.

Tours run weekly in both Kelham Island and the city centre, each stopping off at a handpicked selection of indie favourites – think street food standouts, craft brewers, chocolatiers and off-the-beaten-track gems. Expect five to six stops per tour, with small plates, tasters or drinks at each venue, plus a healthy helping of commentary from your guide on local landmarks, stories and developments along the way.

The Taste of Kelham and Taste of Sheffield tours offer a flavour-packed introduction to each neighbourhood, while the Kelham Food & Beer Tour dives into the area's brewing heritage – visiting five pubs, including The Fat Cat and The Millowners Arms, with a beer at each stop and food served at three of them. For something a little different, the History & Brunch walk adds a side of industrial heritage before rounding off with a sit-down meal.

It's more than just food – it's about celebrating Sheffield's indies and uncovering the stories behind them. With an expanded team of five guides, new tours popping up and options for private parties, corporate bookings and even school visits, there's something for everyone.

Gift vouchers are available too – ideal for birthdays, Christmas or treating that hard-to-buy-for mate or family member. With every ticket supporting a roster of small local businesses – and every tour proudly rated five stars – it's a great way to put your money where your mouth is. Quite literally.

Sheffield Food Tours

@sheffieldfoodtours
sheffieldfoodtours.co.uk

№20
NRY LEAH & SONS
LTD.
CAMBRIDGE
STAMPING WORKS

FOOD
HALL

AMAZELAB

Inspiring curiosity through creativity

Born from a dining room table during lockdown, Amazelab has grown into a pioneering South Yorkshire education company bringing science, technology, engineering, arts and maths to life.

Founded by former teacher and Sheffield-born entrepreneur Leonie Briggs, the organisation was created to make STEAM subjects more accessible, engaging and relevant to everyday life.

Leonie's fascination with science began early. Growing up in the north of Sheffield, she was inspired by local hero Helen Sharman, the first British astronaut to travel to space. Seeing someone from her own city achieve something so extraordinary planted a lifelong belief that science should feel achievable for everyone, regardless of background. That sense of possibility remains central to everything Amazelab does today.

The company delivers workshops across schools, events and community spaces, connecting creativity with practical science to ignite curiosity. Sessions range from exploring how a homemade bat can demonstrate aerodynamics to using colourful Hogwarts-style potions to explain chemistry. By linking learning to imaginations, Amazelab helps children see that science isn't a distant or intimidating subject – it's part of everyday life.

Leonie's background in education and her husband David's design expertise give Amazelab its distinctive look and feel. Together, they create teaching resources, activity packs and large-scale projects that make science visual, playful and inclusive. Their materials are used across the UK and internationally, including work with schools in Jamaica through the British Council.

Partnerships underpin the business. The team collaborates with charities, local authorities and community groups, ensuring that learning remains accessible and meaningful. Leonie also brings Amazelab to public events across Sheffield, running interactive family activities at festivals including Illuminate the Gardens and Pollen Market.

Recognition has followed. Leonie has been named among the UK's top 100 female entrepreneurs and invited to Westminster to share her story of growing a creative business from South Yorkshire. Her first book, *Make Your Own Rainbow: A Colourful Approach to All Things STEAM*, captures Amazelab's philosophy – that creativity and curiosity can open the door to science for everyone.

Rooted in the inventive spirit of its founder's home city, Amazelab shows that discovery doesn't need a laboratory. It starts with imagination, a spark of inspiration and the belief that anyone can reach for the stars.

Amaze Lab
@amaze_lab

amazelab

amazelab

THE LITTLE BOOK OF
SHEFFIELD 2025

LIVE & LOUD

Sheffield's music scene is alive and well – even without its most iconic stage.

Losing The Leadmill was a blow. A legendary space with decades of memories was bound to be a loss but this is Sheffield – a city that doesn't just mourn venues, it builds new scenes. And right now, there are still plenty of stages where you can get your live music fix and the spirit is very much alive.

From sweaty basements to soaring halls, Sheffield's gig landscape covers all bases. At the grassroots end, Sidney and Matilda is a real engine room – a venue that lives and breathes the DIY ethos. Its in-house crew (shoutout to Jarred Up) work tirelessly to platform new talent, and it's become a proper launchpad for Sheffield's next wave and to see the next big thing before they're the thing.

Delicious Clam does it differently – a teeny, offbeat, wonderfully ramshackle spot where scrappy punk, indie and experimental acts let loose. It's run by the artists, for the artists, and feels like the beating heart of the no-rules end of the scene.

There's heritage too. Yellow Arch Studios – once the rehearsal space of the Arctic Monkeys – still packs out with a wildly eclectic programme and keeps its roots in the rehearsal room culture that's long defined this city.

For a gig on the bigger side, Network (formerly Plug) has found new life with backing from the Record Junkee team – a record shop and venue in its own right. Foundry, over at the SU, brings in touring acts with big followings, while next door, the only geometrically significant venue in the city, The Octagon has stepped up as a serious live contender in recent years.

And if it's heavy you're after, Corporation has you covered – Sheffield's long-time home of metal, mosh pits and blue pints. At the other end of the scale, The Washington keeps things casual with free entry shows that are often surprisingly brilliant.

From micro-venues to cavernous spaces, Sheffield still has the volume – and the venues – to back it up.

Photo: @lili_takesflickis

BUSINESS SHEFFIELD

Empowering local enterprise to start, grow and thrive

Business Sheffield is the beating heart of the city's business support network – a service designed to help businesses at every stage, from first idea to steady growth. Part of Sheffield City Council, it provides free, practical guidance to local entrepreneurs, start-ups and established companies, helping them to grow, adapt and succeed.

What makes Sheffield unique as a business city is its scale and character. It's large enough to offer opportunity, yet small enough for collaboration to thrive. That balance, coupled with a deep respect for independent enterprise, has built one of the most supportive business ecosystems in the North. Business Sheffield exists to strengthen that culture, connecting people with advice, funding and resources when they need it most.

Its approach is personal and hands-on. The organisation's specialist advisors bring real-world experience across multiple sectors – from retail and hospitality to manufacturing and tech – offering tailored support through one-to-one sessions, workshops and networking events.

The service is structured around four key teams, each focused on a different part of the business journey. The Launchpad Team helps entrepreneurs and small businesses get off the ground, guiding them through registration, planning, accessing finance, and marketing. The High Street Business Advisors support high street and hospitality businesses, going door to door helping them navigate licensing, planning and environmental health processes along with general business operations.

The Growth Team works with larger and scaling firms on strategy, investment and finance, productivity and innovation. Meanwhile, the Tech Team supports Sheffield's fast-expanding digital and tech community, advising on investment readiness, scaling and collaboration within the local ecosystem.

Beyond individual business support, Business Sheffield also plays a vital role in strengthening the city's economy through strategic projects and initiatives. One of the most significant is the Sheffield Business Directory – a free online platform designed to make it easier for local suppliers to be found. Open to all Sheffield-based companies, it already includes more than 1000 businesses, connecting them to council procurement opportunities and other buyers across the region. The Directory also feeds into the council's Ethical Procurement Policy, ensuring that local firms are fairly represented and that Sheffield's economic growth benefits the people who live and work here.

Beautiful
Blooms

Sheffield
makes

You're in the best city in the UK to start a business*

SEASONAL DRINKS
ICED DRINKS
FRAPPES
MILKSHAKES
COOLERS
TIME for TEA
FOOD ALLERGIES and INTOLERANCES

BUSINESS SHEFFIELD

A commitment to inclusion sits at the heart of Business Sheffield's work. The Diverse Business Advisory Board (DBAB), launched in response to the 2022 Race Equality Commission, works to ensure equitable access to support for underrepresented groups. It champions procurement opportunities for diverse-owned businesses, backs initiatives like See It Be It – which inspires young people across the city – and contributes directly to Sheffield's Future Growth Plan. This work was recognised in 2024 when Business Sheffield received the Equity, Diversity and Inclusion Champion Award at the Sheffield Business Awards.

The organisation also delivers a rolling calendar of events and workshops, both in person and online, covering everything from business planning and digital marketing to AI, HR and finance. Many are led by industry experts and are designed to be accessible, whether you're running a new venture or managing an established enterprise.

From its base at Electric Works, Business Sheffield continues to evolve alongside the city's economy, ensuring that entrepreneurs and business owners have the knowledge, confidence and connections they need. Its mission is simple: to give people the tools to take that next step, whatever stage they're at – and to keep Sheffield's independent spirit thriving for generations to come.

"From the very first day I opened my own Sheffield-based business back in 2013, I've absolutely loved the place. The people of Sheffield are passionate about shopping local and take real pride in all things Steel City.

In my current role with Business Sheffield, my colleagues and I have the privilege of supporting hundreds of local businesses – from helping new ideas take off to guiding established ones as they develop and thrive.

I'd encourage any local independent business to make use of our services. With free workshops, expert advice and hands-on support, we're proud to play a part in helping Sheffield's business community continue to grow and succeed."

Sean Clarke – High Street Business Advisor

Business Sheffield

Business Sheffield
0114 224 5000

businesssheffield
@sheffield.gov.uk
sheffield.gov.uk/business

Closing Remarks

Sheffield Chamber of Commerce
Sheffield makes your plans possible

MEET THE COVER ARTIST: **ROB LEE**

THE ART OF ILLUSION

You'll no doubt have already admired the vibrant, hypnotic cover and motifs that weave their way through the pages of this book (it's probably what led you to pick it up in the first place!). Well, that striking cover is the work of Sheffield-based artist Rob Lee, whose instantly recognisable geometric style has become part of the city's visual fabric. His bold use of pattern, colour and form makes this edition's cover truly stand out – a fitting celebration of Sheffield's creative energy and individuality.

Rob is a multidisciplinary graphic artist specialising in large-scale geometric abstraction. For the past nine years, he has worked full-time as a professional artist, producing countless pieces across private commissions, commercial projects and community murals. His work can be found not only throughout the UK but also in cities around the world, with an ever-growing desire to take his art further afield.

Guided by a deep passion for geometry, pattern, colour and optical illusion, Rob's art explores the relationship between technology, nature and human perception. He often describes himself as being equally inspired by digital precision and organic imperfection, blending the two to create pieces that feel both structured and alive.

A key element of his practice is interaction – he aims to create art that challenges how people see and move through space. His large-scale murals transform walls into moments of presence, offering passers-by a chance to pause, reflect or simply enjoy a splash of colour in their day. He believes deeply in the positive effects public art can have – the power to improve lives, inspire creativity and make people stop and stare for a while.

For Rob, art belongs to everyone. As he puts it, "all boring brick walls should be painted."

robleeart.co.uk | @roblee_art

EVERYONE
HAS
A PART
TO PLAY
Disabled

A Year of Living Curiously

THE LITTLE BOOK OF
SHEFFIELD 2025

ISBN: 978-1-915538-49-9

Compiled by: Emma Toogood & Nick Hallam

Writers: Joe Food & Ash Birch

Photography (unless stated): @marcabarkerphotography

Design: Phil Turner & Marc Barker

Cover Art: Rob Lee

Proofreader: Katie Fisher

Sales and PR: Emma Toogood

Thanks to: Business Sheffield and all the independent businesses that have supported this book.

Published by Meze Publishing Limited
Unit 1b, 2 Kelham Square
Kelham Riverside
Sheffield S3 8SD

Web: www.mezepublishing.co.uk

Telephone: 0114 275 7709

Email: info@mezepublishing.co.uk